Duane Allman

by DAVE RUBIN

Foreword by GALADRIELLE ALLMAN

Recording Credits:

Guitar: Doug Boduch
Keyboards: Warren Wiegratz
Bass: Tom McGirr
Drums: Scott Schroedl

Cover and interior photos: © Amalie R. Rothschild

ISBN 978-1-4234-5870-8

HAL•LEONARD®
CORPORATION

7777 W. BLUEMOUND RD. P.O. BOX 13819 MILWAUKEE, WI 53213

Visit Hal Leonard Online at
www.halleonard.com

A photo of Duane Allman
held by his daughter, Galadrielle

ACKNOWLEDGMENTS

I would like to acknowledge *Skydog*, Richard Poe's excellent biography of Duane Allman published by Backbeat books and distributed by the Hal Leonard Corporation, as a source for some of the biographical information.

DEDICATION

This book is dedicated to John Griffiths, who first alerted me to the power of Duane, and Anthony Mixon, who is a major fan.

FOREWORD

By Galadrielle Allman

There was nothing between my father, Duane Allman, and music: no teacher, no written notation, no fear. You can hear the personal relationship he had with his guitar and the trust he had in his ears and hands. As a young teenager, he committed himself to the guitar with total passion, devoting himself completely to figuring out the guitar's secret language of sounds. It is tempting to think he had a natural and mysterious gift, but his skill was honed by thousands of hours of work. Duane's true gift was his single-minded love of playing; when he played, everything else fell away. What he found was a sound so intimate and specific, that his tone and his approach can be recognized like the inflections of the human voice and its ability to sing, cry, and express true delight or pain.

My father believed that music had the power to bring people together and express the best parts of ourselves. He sought every opportunity to play with other committed and passionate musicians and founded a band of brothers who loved music and needed it as much as he did. With courage, he put himself into situations where a high level of skill was demanded of him, both in sessions and onstage. He loved to play live to crowds. He loved to be tested and to create something new in a moment and share it. He took risks that you can hear. He pushed past what he knew he could do and went further each time, moving within the loose boundaries of a song, finding his own path inside of it. Duane Allman was an explorer and his playing still possesses an immediacy and clarity that lives beyond him—it is magical. The only thing that can soothe the huge pain of losing him is the sound of his playing and the joy he took in it.

If you have this book in your hands, you share Duane's desire to be the best player you can be. Listen to him play and hear what is possible if you really love it. Be inspired by him; don't be content with merely copying him. Commit yourself as he did and express yourself with honesty—beautiful, adventurous music will follow.

Galadrielle Allman is the daughter of Duane and Donna Allman and is currently writing a book about her father.

DUANE ALLMAN: SLIDE DOG

By Dave Rubin

It was said that Duane Allman had an ego "as big as the Grand Canyon," but clearly he also had the outsized talent to fill the enormous void. He was quoted that he could be "up there" after seeing Johnny Winter at the Fillmore East in 1968, and within a year, his boast was made fact. Though the Doors' Robbie Krieger had previously recorded slide guitar in a rock context on "End of the Night" in 1967, Duane's nocturnal stylings on "Dreams," from the Allman Brothers Band two years later, brought traditional blues technique to the forefront of popular music. Of course, it was the context of the blues within the Allman Brothers Band that his impassioned playing plated his reputation as the premier electric bottlenecker of his generation, worthy of taking his place behind Earl Hooker, Elmore James, and Robert Nighthawk as a master of the slashing, single-string slide solo.

Howard Duane Allman was born on November 20, 1946, in Nashville, Tennessee. Brother Gregg was born a little more than a year later on December 8, 1947, and the first of many tragedies for the Allman brothers occurred when their father, Willis, an Army sergeant, was murdered by a fellow veteran in 1949. In short order, their mother, Geraldine "Mama A." Allman, packed up the family to stay with relatives. In 1957, after Duane and Gregg had spent two years at Castle Heights Military Academy, the family relocated to Daytona, Florida. On one of their visits back to Nashville to see their grandmother, Gregg was taught "She'll Be Comin' 'Round the Mountain When She Comes" on guitar by a neighbor, and when he returned home, he pestered his mother to get him one. Saving up money from his paper route and with some extra financial assistance from his mother, he purchased a Sears Silvertone Flat-top acoustic.

After trashing his Harley-Davidson 165 Motorbike, Duane began coveting both the axe and his little brother's fledgling chops. They fought over the prize, with Duane sneaking into Gregg's room and playing the instrument uninvited, but not without having Gregg show him his first chords—including the I, IV, and V changes in the key of E. Eventually, Duane was given his own guitar (to "keep the peace") and the brothers started playing together. Meanwhile, he also greatly benefited from his relationship with guitarist Jim Shepley, a much more advanced player a few years older, whom Duane had boldly met at the pool room in 1958. When Shepley showed Duane the basic Jimmy Reed boogie patterns, the die was cast. Further fuel was added to Duane's starting fire when he and Gregg saw B.B. King in concert during a summer trip to Nashville, prompting Duane to exclaim, "Little brother, we've got to get into this." They both continued learning, but Duane threw himself into practicing day and night. By 1960, Gregg had gone electric with a Fender Musicmaster and Duane followed suit with a 1959 Les Paul Junior (to "keep the peace"), and in 1963, they formed their first band, the Shufflers, with Duane singing and Gregg playing lead. Duane eventually became so obsessed with the guitar at the expense of his schooling that he ended up back at the military academy for a while before finally quitting altogether. He urged Gregg to do the same, but the younger boy did not possess the same unshakable confidence and stayed with his studies, graduating from public high school in 1965 and planning to become a dentist.

The two Allman brothers formed other bands while performing Stones, Beatles, and Yardbirds tunes up and down Daytona Beach as the Escorts and then the Allman Joys, with whom they presciently cut versions of "Spoonful" and "Crossroads" around 1966. It was at this time that Duane fell under the spell of Cream and other heavy

British blues-rockers. After Gregg graduated, he planned to allot just a year to the full-time music gig that Duane desired, after which he planned to attend college and dental school, but the year stretched on a bit longer than planned. They changed their name to the Hour Glass and their music evolved from rock to soul to pop. With assistance and encouragement from the Nitty Gritty Dirt Band, Duane and Gregg snared a contract with Liberty Records in California, headed west, and recorded two albums. The sand quickly ran out for the Hour Glass, however, when the label nixed their idea to record a third album of the blues and R&B they craved.

While in California, Duane got sick, so Gregg did him a good turn that would have far reaching results for him personally and for the history and development of rock and electric blues. He bought him Taj Mahal's first album which included a cover of Blind Willie McTell's "Statesboro Blues" with Ry Cooder playing slide, that would have a profound influence on the version ending up on *Live at the Fillmore East*. Inspired to play slide, Duane just happened to use the Coricidin bottle that had contained his cold medicine as his slider, and a unique style was born. Gregg decided to stay in California and try his luck while Duane turned back towards home. On the way, he found himself in Muscle Shoals, Alabama, where he scored session work with Boz Scaggs, Otis Rush, Aretha Franklin, and Wilson Pickett in 1968. Perhaps not coincidentally, each session that his presence graced turned out to be a landmark. With Scaggs, he soloed heroically on the epic version of Fenton Robinson's "Somebody Loan Me a Dime." Rush's *Mourning in the Morning*, produced by Mike Bloomfield and Nick Gravenites, was a valiant but failed attempt to bring the legendary Chicago blues guitarist to a wider audience, but it includes a stellar performance by Duane on "Reap What You Sow." He was there "at the creation" when he played on the Queen of Soul's "I Never Loved a Man (The Way I Love You)" and "Do Right Woman, Do Right Man" breakthrough sessions. Most significantly, however, it was his stunning work with Wilson Pickett on "Hey Jude" that set forces in motion and helped change the direction of rock music to embracing blues, soul, and R&B music. When Pickett came to Muscle Shoals at the behest of Atlantic Records to get his share of the magic emanating from Rick Hall's studio, he was presented with a different type of session guitarist than what he was used to. Hall related the story about the fabulous mystery soloist on the revolutionary track to Atlantic Records producer extraordinaire, Jerry Wexler (the man who is often credited with coining the term "rhythm & blues"), as "Hey Jude" was becoming a million seller: "Wilson calls him 'Sky Man' 'cause he likes to get high. He's got hair down to his butt. He's a hippie from Macon, but I'll be damned if he didn't talk Pickett into singing the song. Wilson said a Beatles tune didn't fit him. The hippie said, 'What's wrong, you don't got the balls to sing it?' That's all Pickett needed to hear." Jerry Jemmott, the premier R&B session bass man on the dates, also had a story to tell from the occasion: "it seems that the 'Wicked Pickett' was driving his rhythm section back to their hotel one night and Duane started to sit in the front seat. Pickett stopped the long-haired hippie and requested that he sit in the back, saying that he did not want people (in the Southern town) to think he had 'some white woman in the car with him!'" In time, Duane's nickname evolved to "Skydog" due to his scruffy red beard or his propensity for getting high, depending on who is telling the story.

Wexler was so knocked out by Duane's melodically soulful blues, advanced chops, and versatility that he bought his contract from Hall and put him with Delaney Bramlett, among others. In England, another white blues phenom was also mightily impressed. When he came to the States to record in 1970, Eric Clapton would ask to meet Duane and have him play on his session.

Before that, in 1969, Duane was chafing to get his own band together. Despite his success and accolades from the various Muscle Shoals sessions, he returned to Jacksonville, Florida. A short stint in the Second Coming with Dickey Betts and Berry Oakley gave him access to a second lead guitarist and a sympathetic bassist. He added the tandem drummers Butch Trucks and Jaimoe (Johnny Lee Johnson) Johanson and convened an epochal jam. Buzzed with the possibilities but lacking a lead singer, Duane summoned Gregg back from Los Angeles. Little brother was miserable doing grossly inappropriate material with Southern California studio pros, so he hitchhiked home. When he arrived at the first rehearsal, he was intimidated by the power of the assembled musicians, but a run through of Muddy Waters' "Trouble No More" convinced him and everyone else that Duane's dream band was ready to rock the blues. Within a week, Gregg composed "Black-Hearted Woman" and "Whipping Post."

The Allman Brothers Band signed with the newly created Capricorn Records and went on the road in Florida and Georgia before ducking into the studio for their first album. The eponymous release in 1969 was not an immediate commercial success, selling less than 50,000 copies. Reviews were positive, however, and the group attracted a following that would grow. Their seamless blending of blues and rock with elements of jazz improvisation set them apart from the other nascent blues-rock outfits of the era. Gregg's raspy vocals had the ring of authenticity and the twin-lead guitar harmonies of Duane and Dickey, not heard since the heyday of western swing in the 1940s, gave them a readily identifiable signature sound. The band soon became known for their marathon concert jams as Dickey fretted along with Duane, who bottlenecked the audience into ecstasy over the mammoth groove of the muscular rhythm section, that included Gregg's vibrant Hammond B3 organ pads and the two drummers.

In 1970, the ABB began work in Macon, Georgia, on their second offering, *Idlewild South*, with former Cream producer Tom Dowd. During the course of the sessions, Eric Clapton's manager called to inform Dowd that his client wanted to come to Florida to record with his new band, Derek & the Dominos. When Dowd relayed the news to Duane, the Allman brother asked if he could stop by to watch one of his idols in action. Then, when the Brothers were scheduled to play a gig in Miami that summer, Clapton was anxious to see the cat who scared the wits out of him with his playing on "Hey Jude" and he attended the show with Dowd. Though Duane freaked out when he saw Clapton down front, the entire band went back to Criteria Studios afterwards for an all-night jam.

When it came time for "Eric" & the Dominos to record *Layla and Other Assorted Love Songs*, Duane was all set to watch when "Slowhand" insisted that he also play. What started out to be a "guest" appearance on a couple of tracks ended up as a full-scale collaboration on the entire album. All parties involved agreed that Duane's presence spurred Clapton (an occasional underachiever) to extend himself beyond the usual, and his contribution to the immortal title track cannot be underestimated. Duane would always consider the album some of his best playing, and few would argue that it represents some of the greatest blues and blues-rock wailing ever committed to tape. Clapton was so gassed that he invited Duane to join the Dominos. He demurred to remain with the Brothers, but it is rumored, though not confirmed, that he did play out with the group for a number of shows.

Idlewild South showed a greater depth of material with acoustic tunes like Gregg's "Midnight Rider" and Dickey Betts' jazzy masterpiece, "In Memory of Elizabeth Reed." Out on the road, the Brothers were building a reputation as a performance band without peer, stretching improvisations to 30 minutes and more. In March of 1971, they played a week at the Fillmore East in New York City that was recorded, mixed, and released as a double album that fall. Though snobbish fans would sometimes comment that it represented the ABB on just an "average" night, it has come to be regarded as one of the greatest live albums in history. Their version of T-Bone Walker's "Stormy Monday," via Bobby Blue Bland's 1961 rendition, has become the standard against which all subsequent covers are measured. The album went gold on October 15, but on October 29, 24-year-old Duane was killed on his Harley-Davidson Sportster XLCH chopper in Macon, GA.

The band was about halfway through *Eat a Peach*, their third studio album, when this tragedy occurred, so they completed the recording with Betts finishing up the remaining guitar tracks. Duane was prominently featured on the majority of tunes, however, including "Mountain Jam" (based on Donovan's "First There Is a Mountain"), which covered one complete disc of the double album. Duane's pyromaniacal slide on Sonny Boy Williamson's "One Way Out" would help to make it, similar to "Stormy Monday," the benchmark for all future versions, and his "Little Martha," along with Betts' "Blue Sky," would also become ABB classics. The LP became the band's first to break into the Top 10 at #4. During the course of cutting the follow-up to *Eat a Peach*, Berry Oakley also died in a motorcycle accident on November 12, 1972, not far from where Duane crashed. The group would continue on with one guitarist and Chuck Leavell on keyboards until Dan Toler arrived in 1978, and then Warren Haynes (current lead guitarist) filled the second guitar chair 10 years later. Young buck Derek Trucks, nephew of Brother Butch, was added as a full-time member in 1999. The ABB continues to roll on into the 21st century despite having fired Dickey Betts for irreconcilable differences in 2000 after 30 years of living and surviving the blues together.

Duane Allman brought his immense passion for the blues, fired with the energy of rock and the improvisational depth of jazz, to create a legacy on slide guitar that endures undiminished. In three short years with his Allman Brothers Band, he used his guitar to eloquently express his unique and original instrumental poetry that will always speak volumes to all who fall under its hypnotic spell.

DUANE ALLMAN GEAR

After the 1959 Les Paul Junior Double Cutaway he got in 1960, Duane acquired a 1956/57 Fender Stratocaster. While with the Allman Joys, he played a mid-1960s Gibson ES-335 with block inlays and a Bigsby vibrato unit. During the same period, he also had a Fender Telecaster with a Stratocaster neck—a modification that Eric Clapton also tried while with Blind Faith. Duane first played both guitars through a Vox Super Beatle amp and then a Fender Twin Reverb amp. At Muscle Shoals, he used a post-CBS Strat with a rosewood fingerboard through a Twin and a Fuzz Face stomp box, though he also had a 1961 pre-CBS model with a rosewood neck.

Duane is most famous for playing Les Pauls and his first was a 1957 Gold Top that he used on the first two ABB albums, and likely "Layla." Both he and Clapton recorded through tiny, 6-watt Fender Champ amps. Shortly thereafter, Duane traded the Gold Top for a circa-1958 Les Paul Cherry Sunburst after slyly having the pickups swapped out. In 1970 he was seen with a circa-1958 Gibson ES-335 Dot Neck, and in 1971 he played a 1961 Gibson Les Paul/SG standard in New York. That same year he acquired his iconic circa-1959 Tobacco Burst Les Paul Standard. This is the axe that Gibson copied for their Duane Allman Signature Edition reissue and is now owned by Galadrielle Allman, who has loaned it to the Rock and Roll Hall of Fame. With the Brothers, Duane played through two 50-watt Marshall bass heads with Marshall Bass 100 cabinets. For acoustics, Duane had a 1937–39 National Duolian resonator and a late 1930s/early 1940s Gibson L-00.

BLUE SKY

(*Eat a Peach*, 1972)
Words and Music by Dickey Betts

The first Allman Brothers album released, post-Duane, was also their top charter to date (#4), no doubt due in large degree to Duane's enormous contributions to the live cuts and studio tracks. The single "Blue Sky" was written by Dickey about his Native American girlfriend, Sandy "Bluesky" Wabegijig, that he married in 1973 and with whom he had a daughter named "Jessica." Following his divorce from Bluesky in 1975 and Duane's death, Dickey refused to play the tender, melancholy song for years afterward.

Figure 1—Intro

The melodic, "smooth as a Georgia peach" intro is an excellent "introduction" to the great tandem guitars of Duane and Dickey. It also shows how Duane could play an appropriate accompaniment part as well as being the "big engine that pulls the train." Dickey (Gtr. 1) sets the vibe for the entire song when he starts off with an undulating, ascending line derived from the E major pentatonic scale voiced in the root position of the C# minor pentatonic scale in measures 1–4. Duane (Gtr. 2) follows suit in the same fret position with a complimentary pattern utilizing double stops in 3rds and 4ths resulting in a full, fat harmony. In measures 5–6, Dickey implies the I (E) and ♭VII (D) chords with 3rds and a broken D major triad, respectively. Reversing roles, Duane takes the opposite tack by playing a single-note line from the E major scale, albeit combined with the open high-E string as a pedal tone, that follows the I, ♭VII, and IV (A) changes.

Performance Tip: For Gtr. 2, barre with the index finger at fret 9 in measure 1 and 3 while accessing the A note at fret 10 with the middle finger. To play the dyads in measure 2 and 4, execute the small barres with the index, ring, middle and index fingers, and index, from high to low.

Figure 2—Guitar Solo (Measures 1–32)

Despite being the composer and lead singer of the song, Dickey graciously allows Duane (Gtr. 2) the courtesy of taking the first solo. He responds, over 32 measures of the I (E) and IV (A) chord changes with the E major pentatonic scale in the root position of C♯ minor pentatonic, functioning as the relative minor of E, with the occasional addition of the A note on string 2, fret 10. This distinctive and highly versatile form is also called the *major hexatonic scale*, due to its six notes, and it is a "major" component in the styles of the brothers Allman. The beauty of the scale is the equal relationship to both the I and IV chords it has that the relative minor pentatonic scale does not. This improvisational approach was a hallmark of both Duane and Dickey when soloing over modal vamps in other ABB non-blues songs ("Melissa" and "Midnight Rider"). The reasons for that choice are simple and logical: besides the root, 2nd, 3rd, 5th, and 6th notes of the major scale that are found in the major pentatonic scale, the major hexatonic scale includes the critical 4th degree so important when playing songs or progressions with I and IV chords.

Figure 2 is a highly instructive example of how to play a *modal solo* (a solo where one scale is utilized to play over all of the changes). In this case, as the progression is a two-measure, two-chord vamp, the overriding tonality is E major and Duane mainly proceeds accordingly with his note choice. However, early on, he tacitly acknowledges the change to the IV (A) chord in measure 4 and briefly drops down into the major hexatonic box (below the root position), to access the root (A) at fret 7 on string 4. Likewise, in measures 12 and 18 of the IV chord, he emphasizes the root and major 7th (G♯) notes, and in measure 16 he leans on the 9th (B) and major 3rd (C♯) to help indicate the A tonality. These are exceptions to the rule, however, because in the rest of the solo, he gets in his tone and phrasing "zone," where his enormous skills are used to create wave after wave of musical tension and release while increasing intensity to rivet the listener's attention.

One of his "signature licks" is in the root position of the relative minor scale, where he bends the G string from the 2nd (or 9th) to the tonality-defining major 3rd. Occurring straight off in measures 1–3 (F♯ bend to G♯), it is employed throughout as a motif, often followed by the E, functioning as the root of the I chord for resolution or as the 5th of the IV chord for mild musical tension.

Observe how measures 22–24 signify peak intensity and tension, and the climax of the solo, as Duane repeats a dizzying series of 16th- and 32nd-note hammer-ons and pull-offs involving mainly just the G♯, A, and E notes over the IV–I–IV chords at the 16th position. Quite brilliantly, the notes chosen to harmonize with the E (I) and A (IV) chords are contained in the major scales of both keys that produce palpable musical tension by virtue of the fast, repetitive phrasing. Measure 25 of the I chord actually continues with a galvanizing display of peak energy, as Duane works his way down string 2 with a descending run utilizing E major scale notes. It begins with the E as a continuation of the same notes from the previous measure of the IV chord, and then ends on E in anticipation of measure 26 of the IV chord. In measures 29–32 of the I, IV, I, and IV chords, Duane creates a two-measure melodic line in the extension position, or "Albert King box," of the C♯ minor pentatonic scale. This repeats twice and serves to complete his solo with a memorable motif, rather than going out with a big, improvisational bang.

Performance Tip: For the repeating licks in measures 22–24, use the index finger for the G♯ at fret 16 on string 1, and the middle finger for the A note at fret 17 on string 1 as well as the E note at fret 17 on string 2.

Fig. 2

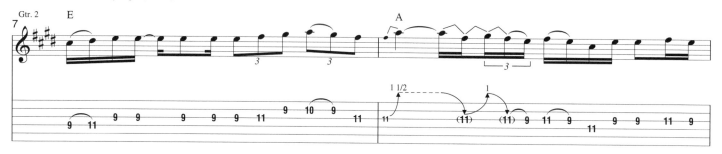

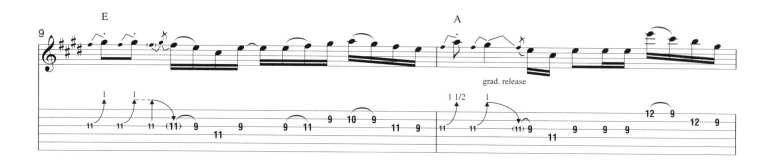

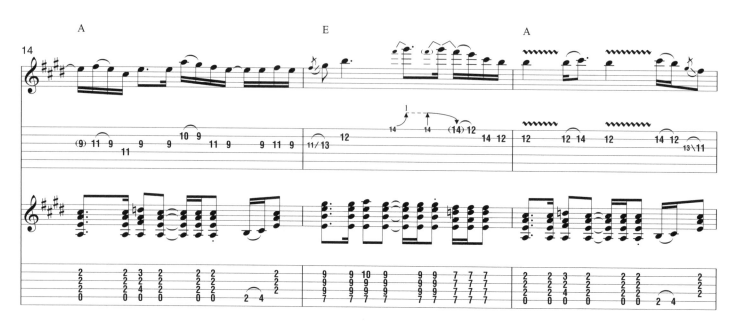

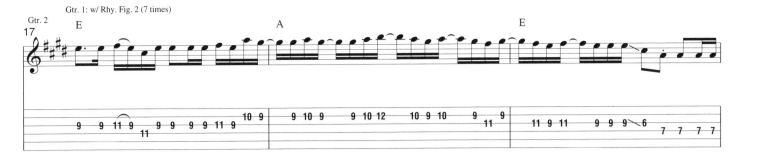

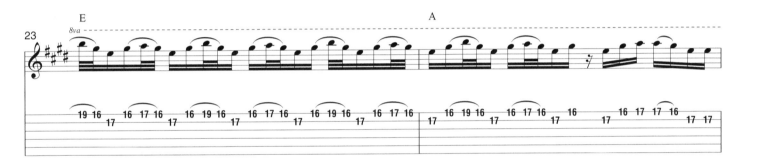

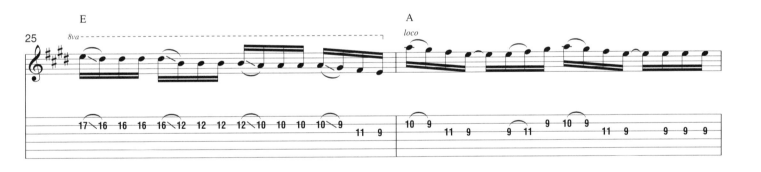

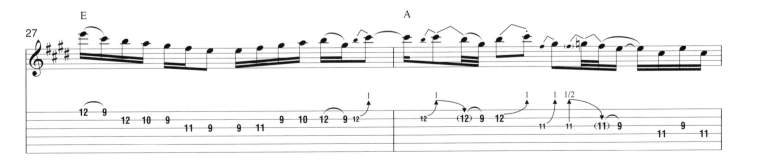

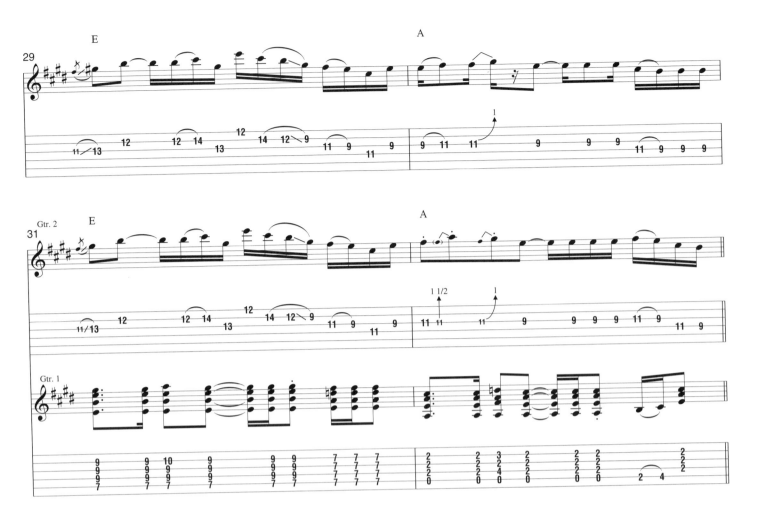

Figure 3—Guitar Solo (Measures 33–36)

The tail end of Duane's solo could be seen as an interlude that connects to Dickey's solo (not shown). The four measures of I–IV–I–IV (E–A–E–A) changes afford the opportunity for the two "pick meisters" to display their signature twin-lead guitar melody lines that are still thrilling to hear, even after being recorded 35 years ago. Without skipping a beat, Dickey (Gtr. 1) repeats Duane's "melody" from measures 29–32 as a brilliant transition. At the same time, Duane (Gtr. 2) seamlessly changes registers to play the harmony, mainly at the 16th position of the C♯ minor pentatonic scale (or E major pentatonic), with a combination of mostly 4th, 5th, and 6th intervals. Dickey has commented that Duane was intuitive about his choices and sometimes even played "wrong" notes that somehow fit. That does not occur here, though it is interesting to observe that on beat 4 of measures 33 and 34, he plays the same note (E) as Dickey, only an octave higher. Being a minor detail, it appears to be a "happy accident," subtly going outside the "system" of playing 4ths, 5ths, and 6ths—a somewhat random result of Duane playing the same scale as Dickey, but in a higher position on the fretboard.

Performance Tip: Slide into the C♯ note on string 3 at fret 18 with the middle finger; this should put you in an advantageous position to access the E note on string 2 at fret 17 with the index finger and the F♯ note on the same string at fret 19 with the ring finger. Note that the index should also be used for the G♯ note on string 1 at fret 16 and the middle finger for the A note one fret higher on beat 2 of measures 33 and 35.

Fig. 3

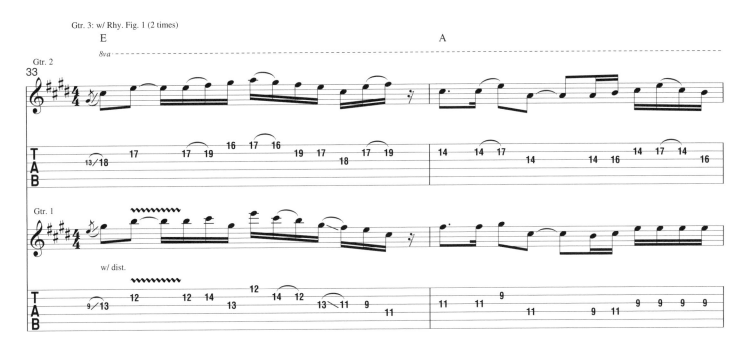

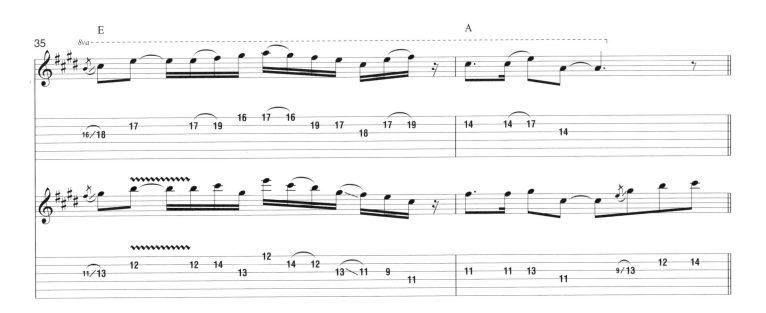

DREAMS I'LL NEVER SEE

(*The Allman Brothers Band*, 1969)
Words and Music by Gregg Allman

Dickey Betts recalls that Duane was the most proud of his work on this epic Allman Brothers classic. Duane described it as, "Dreams..." is the effect that good jazz had on us. If you can get the music flowing out there where you don't have to listen to it, it just takes you away." Written by Gregg while he was still in California, he remembers it as the only song he ever wrote on the Hammond B3 organ and as the first song the band learned all the way through in 1969 after he returned to Jacksonville, Florida. At over seven minutes, it is the longest track on their debut album and a certifiable landmark of blues-rock.

Figure 4—Intro

Following four measures of organ, bass, and drums implying an ambiguous D major vamp, Duane (Gtr. 1) tightens up the structure by alternating D (root) and A (5th) whole notes for the four measures preceding the verse (not shown). Simple yet elegant, it establishes the fact that there is a two-chord vamp with two subtly different chord changes, though they are not actually revealed until the guitar solo. Observe that Duane plays the D note in measure 3 an octave above the one in measure 1 for variety.

Performance Tip: Use the index finger for all four notes.

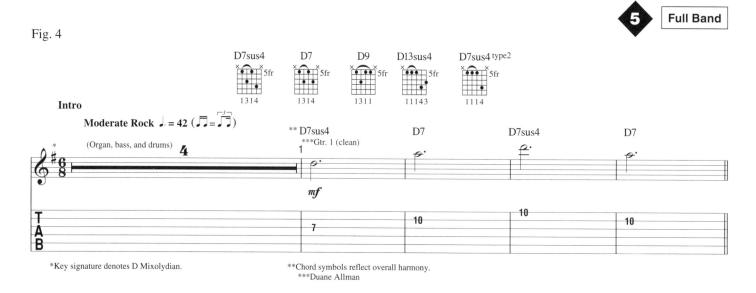

Fig. 4

*Key signature denotes D Mixolydian.   **Chord symbols reflect overall harmony.
***Duane Allman

Figure 5—Guitar Solo

Duane (Gtr. 1) begins this worthy monument to his talent by soloing modally over the I-chord vamp of D11–D7 with the D major pentatonic scale in several positions. Be aware that he sometimes adds the 4th (G) to the root (D), 2nd (E), 3rd (F♯), 5th (A), and 6th (B) notes to form a D major hexatonic scale. Throughout, Duane employs the G note for color as in measure 9, or for musical tension in measure 11 where he bends the ♭3rd (F) to the 4th. In measures 13–15, however, he expands his tonal palette even further by dynamically dropping to the 4th position and adding the ♭7th (C) note where it combines with the 6th (B) for melodic purposes. It also functions as the "leading tone" of D dominant (D7), even though Duane chooses to play it over the D11 voicing where it imparts a smoky, bluesy flavor not as evident in most of the solo.

Check out that Duane is in no hurry to jack up the tension or energy, so he leaves estimable chops in reserve while plumbing the depths of his emotions through his beefy Les Paul that sonically resembles a saxophone. In keeping with the "dreams" theme of the song, he floats along over the backing track as if on an electric cloud until measure 19, where swooping two-step bends from the 4th to the 6th (B) set up a series of half-, whole-, and 1-1/2-step bends that bring in measure 21. In measures 22–24, he moves up the fingerboard with smooth, controlled power to the 14th position of the D major hexatonic scale, peaking with intensity and sweet, singing bends from the 5th (A) to the 6th (B). Between measures 25–30, Duane dynamically shifts down the neck through several positions of the scale, bottoming out in measures 28–29 in open position with strings 5 (A) and 4 (D), functioning as the 5th and root, respectively. Starting in measure 30, he arcs upward and peaks around the 14th position in measures 33–34, before resolving to the root (D) in measure 36 with long sustain, teetering on the edge of feedback. It is a potent gesture that foretells even more dramatic and expressive improvisation to come.

Performance Tip: All bends should be executed with the ring finger backed up by the middle and index fingers, if practical. This is especially recommended for the multi-step bends.

Fig. 5

6 Full Band

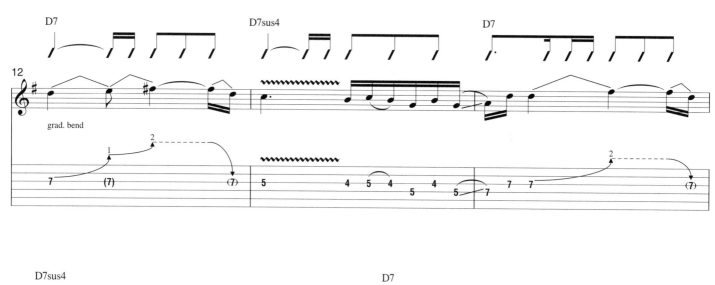

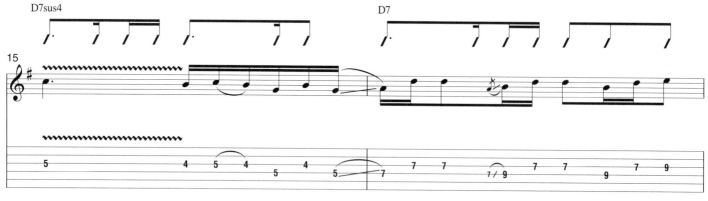

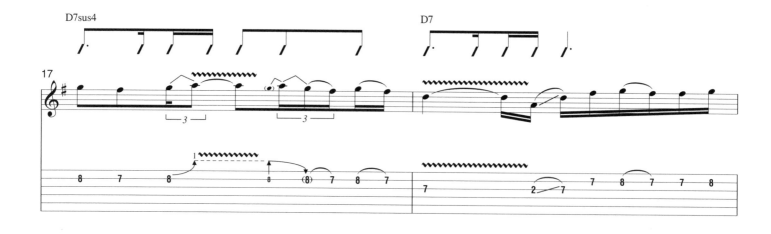

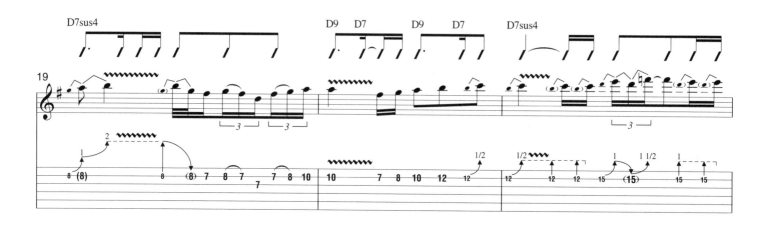

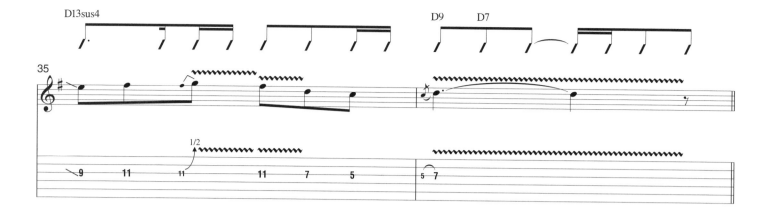

Figure 6—Guitar Solo (Slide)

With the sustained note (D) of the previous measure (Figure 6) buying him some time, in the blink of an eye, Duane slips the Coricidin bottle on his ring finger and vibratos the ♭7th (C) leading tone at fret 5 on string 3 into controlled feedback, thereby fluidly initiating the beginning of his second solo that flows like liquid gold. What follows is a magnificent display of virtuosic slide technique, tamed and harnessed in the service of musical artistry of the highest order. This artistry encompasses a rich variety of musical ideas that could, and would, be further explored in concert. For example, in measures 1–7 he invents melodies on the upper strings in the D *composite blues scale* (Mixolydian mode plus blues scale) with prime notes "singled" out for emphasis via slippery vibrato. Notice how in measures 1–4, the ♭7th (C), root (D), 4th (G), and root are sequenced to beautifully illustrate the concept of alternating tension and release in a modal solo. In measures 5–7 (including beat 1 of measure 8) he opts to produce musical tension with the ♭7th, 5th (A), and 4th notes as a means to increase energy and anticipation for measures 8 and 9 where he repeats convoluted triplets consisting of the root, major 7th (C♯), and 5th scale degrees as a mini-climax. Measures 10 and 11 contain resolution introduced by the tonality-defining major 3rd (F♯), followed by repetition of the root.

Measure 12 signals a change away from solitary melody lines towards harmony for a dynamic and textural shift that is a surprising and unique approach in the realm of blues and rock slide guitar. Duane begins with a broken D major triad in measure 12 followed by a raked and arpeggiated D11 triple stop in measure 13. The two measures are a tease and preview of what will become the big harmonic climax of the solo, but first Duane decides to dynamically contrast the chordal forms with two measures of melody, utilizing the major 3rd, 4th, 5th, and ♭7th notes of the D Mixolydian mode to impart a decidedly dominant tone. Starting in measure 17 and continuing through measure 28 (save for measure 24 of single notes for dynamics), however, Duane composes a remarkable series of broken triads and triple stops in two octaves that provide nothing less than the sonic equivalent of a horn section. Measures 22 and 23 are similar to measures 12 and 13, but, along with measures 25–28, contain nonuplets (groups of nine) in place of three eighth notes. The extraordinary result is one of building momentum, and is also incontrovertible evidence of the tremendous accuracy of his slide and effectiveness of his damping technique. After trailing off from the D major triad in measure 28 and leaving a half-measure rest, Duane cools down in measures 29–32 with D and A whole notes similar to the intro, leaving welcome breathing room after the compressed energy of the previous measures, before the upcoming verse (not shown).

Performance Tip: Remember that Duane is using the bare fingers of his right hand to pick and pluck the strings when playing slide. For the triads and triple stops, try a pattern of thumb, index, and middle fingers on strings 4, 3, and 2, respectively.

Fig. 6

Dreams I'll Never See

Dreams I'll Never See

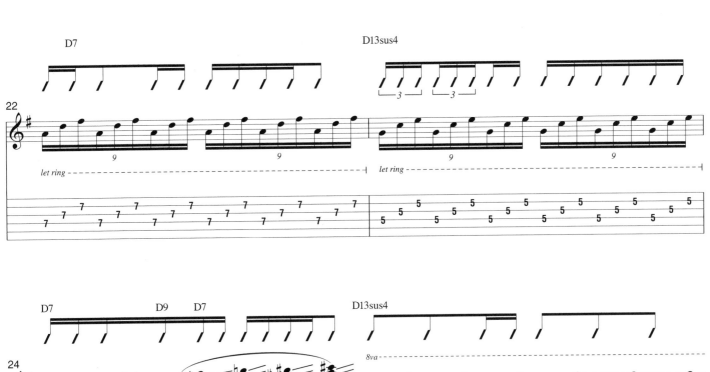

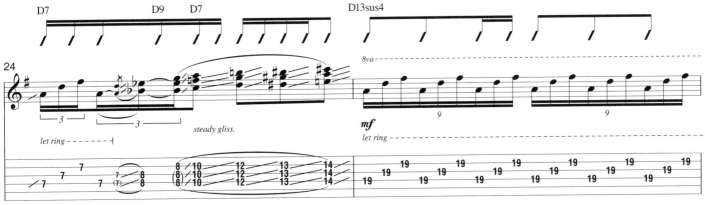

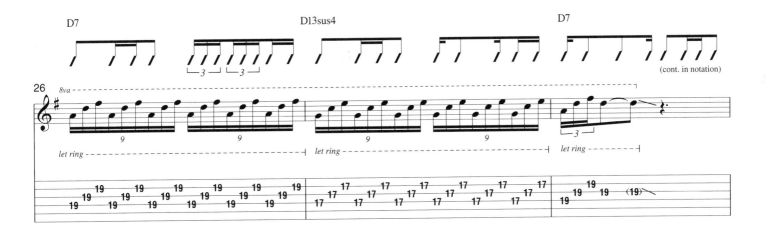

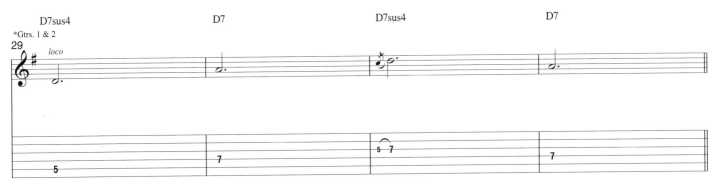

*Gtr. 1 w/o slide

Figure 7—Outro

Employing the same descending and dramatic two-measure, twin-guitar harmony pattern first heard in the interlude (not shown) and the outro, Duane and Dickey (Gtr. 2) repeat it through the fade. Gtr. 2 plays the "melody" in the D Mixolydian mode, while Gtr. 1 harmonizes below in 4ths, 3rds, and 5ths. Check out the "wrong" harmony of C against Dickey's F# on beat 2 in measures 2 and 4. That is a dissonant, but "bluesy" ♭5th! Also, be aware of the striking aural effect that results when both guitarists bend in unison. Because there are almost always slight discrepancies in the speed and pitch of bending, a vibrant, shimmering quality occurs that lends a subtle, but exciting, "organic" feel that would be absent in double-tracked harmonies done by a single guitarist.

Performance Tip: Execute all bends and vibrato with the ring finger by pushing up and pulling down, respectively.

Fig. 7

Dreams I'll Never See

IN MEMORY OF ELIZABETH REED

(At Fillmore East, 1971)
By Dickey Betts

Nowhere is the Allman Brothers' jazz influence more pronounced than in Dickey Betts' epic improvisational jam based loosely on Miles Davis's "All Blues." He titled it after a name he saw on a headstone at the Rose Hill Cemetery in Macon, Georgia, where he would often go to write. (He did not want to reveal the real-live woman it was about for fear of getting shot by her jealous man.) A fan and critic's favorite, this version was actually recorded seven months before appearing on *Idlewild South* in 1970. It was the first of several original instrumentals penned by Dickey to prominently feature Duane. The album, long heralded as one of the greatest live recordings in rock music history, hit #13 on the pop charts.

Figure 8—A Section (Intro)

Duane is rightly honored and revered (some would say worshipped!) as a lead guitar god, but he was a complete guitarist that could do it all. The four-measure intro shows a modest example (Gtr. 1) of his rhythm chops. You should know that these top-string forms are a staple of R&B and soul guitar and were perhaps acquired during his Muscle Shoals' days, backing the likes of Wilson Pickett and Aretha Franklin. Also observe that the Am9 (vi9) voicing could also be read as a Cma7 (I) chord and the D6 (II) as Bm7 (vii7) where they would function as the relative major and relative minor chords, respectively.

Performance Tip: Play the Am9 with the pinky, ring, middle, and index fingers, low to high. Barre the Am and D6 voicings with the index finger.

Fig. 8

Figure 9—Sections E and F

"In Memory of Elizabeth Reed" contains some of the most extensive and expansive twin-guitar harmony lines found anywhere in the Allman Brothers catalog. Sections E and F combined are "signature" of the multi-part "head" of the tune and are particularly choice examples of Duane and Dickey's art. Section E is eight measures long consisting of vi (Am), vi, vi, vi, i (Cm), i, vi, and vi chords. Dickey (Gtr. 2) plays the top melody in measures 1–4 that could be seen to be derived from the root position of the A Aeolian mode, though in reality it is just the A minor pentatonic scale with the addition of the 2nd (B) note to form a *minor hexatonic* scale. Duane (Gtr. 1) responds simultaneously in the root position of the A minor pentatonic scale, basically one string below Dickey. The result mainly produces harmonies in 5ths. In measures 5–6, they both relocate to the root position of the C minor hexatonic and C minor pentatonic scales, respectively. Measures 7–8 contain a virtual duplicate of Gtrs. 1 and 2 from measures 1–2. Be sure to pay attention to the fact that Duane never plays his patterns in a completely parallel fashion to Dickey, and therein lies his (intuitive) genius. For instance, in measure 2 where Dickey plays G (♭7th), B (2nd), and G in beats 1 and 2, Duane plays E, G, and D, functioning as the 3rd, 6th, and 4th. If he had played the parallel pattern of C, F♯, and C, it would have resulted in parallel 5ths, as are most of the Duane/Dickey harmonies.

Section F is five measures long over an implied Am tonality. Dickey contributes a two-measure melodic riff played twice that appears to be derived from the A *melodic minor* scale consisting of the root (A), 2nd (B), ♭3rd (C), 4th (D), 5th (E), 6th (F♯), and 7th (G♯) notes. His prominent inclusion of the G♯ note on string 2 at fret 9 in measures 9–12 is a defining characteristic of his line as well as the melodic minor scale. Meanwhile, Duane (Gtr. 1), follows along with his typical parallel 5ths on beats 1–3 of measures 9 and 10. However, over beat 4 in each measure he plays sweeter 6th intervals to keep the lines from being so predictable in sound. Notice how the 5ths, especially in half steps, contribute to the "Eastern" flavor of Section F.

When Dickey skips down the melodic minor scale from the root (A) in measure 13 on the way to resolution on the V7 (E7♯9) chord, he adds the bluesy ♭5th (E♭) for "grit," as Duane improvises his usual hip harmony with 5ths and 6ths for a sophisticated riff that jazz cats would be proud to have created.

Performance Tip: For both guitars in Section F, play all the vibratoed notes with your index finger and access the bend with your pinky backed up by the ring, middle, and index, if time permits.

Fig. 9

Figure 10—Section ☐ (Guitar Solo)

Duane produced one of the crowning moments of his career during this 128 measures of spectacular rock-jazz improvisation. It alone would assure his reserved seating in the pantheon of the greats. A comparison with the tenor sax jazz giant John Coltrane that some have made may be a bit of a stretch, but Duane's aggressive, uninhibited approach to improvising outside of a blues or rock context clearly had more to do with the free-flowing jazz sensibility of the late sixties than the vast majority of the era's rock music. Only Michael Bloomfield and Jimi Hendrix would occasionally venture with confidence into the territory that would later come to be called fusion.

The late, legendary Who drummer, Keith Moon, once quipped that the entrance and exit of a solo was all people remembered, but Duane must have been absent the day "Professor" Moon gave that lecture as he never lets up for one beat from beginning to end. He solos (Gtr. 1) over the same i9–IV6 (Am9–D6), one-measure vamp that both Dickey and Brother Gregg had at their disposal, and comes in blazing in an impressive show of instrumental strength in measures 1–24. Inhabiting the root and extension positions of the A minor pentatonic scale, he employs a great number of sixteenth notes for energy and propulsive momentum while hewing close to the accepted method of modal improvisation by creating "alternating currents" (in both meanings of the term!) of musical tension and resolution. However, since the root (A) as his note of resolution is integrated into his "sheets of sound" approach, there is virtually no release from the immense musical tension generated until measures 25–28. There, Duane eases up with looping bends and vibrato, though he still studiously avoids the root. In measures 29–31, he transitions to the next movement of his six-string symphony with slower melodic lines that hint at the appropriate A *Dorian mode* by adding the 2nd (B) to the A minor pentatonic fingering and avoids resolution to the root in order to maintain a degree of tension and anticipation.

Measures 32–40 find Duane more firmly involved in the root position of the A Dorian mode with his inclusion of the 6th (F♯) in addition to the 2nd. He rolls back his volume (and hence, distortion) and dances on the strings percussively in a highly syncopated and swinging manner that contrasts with the two previous sections of his solo that contained long, fluid sustain. He also includes the root more frequently so as not to encourage tonal ambiguity, though still not at the point of releasing the accumulating musical tension that he has been fostering since the beginning of this long journey of musical discovery.

Duane flows smoothly into his next section of measures 41–48 where he cranks his volume back up and focuses his attention on flowing horizontal licks, dynamically restricted to the beefy bass strings, up and down the fingerboard in the A Aeolian mode, making sure to play the potent ♭6th (F, as opposed to the 6th [F♯] of the Dorian mode) only against the Am9, rather than the D6 where it would clash with the major 3rd (F♯). With sax-like tone and phrasing, he changes the playing field without sacrificing his passion to explore the possibilities of improvisation, no matter where it may lead. In measures 49–66, his curiosity takes him mainly back to the root and extension positions of the A Dorian mode where he builds compressed tension with twisting, serpentine licks, runs, and jackhammer hits on the A, functioning as the root of Am9 and the 5th of D6. As he becomes totally immersed in the driving momentum of his fusillade of notes, Duane makes a transition to the 12th position of the A minor pentatonic scale beginning in measure 67, continues on to measure 76 with the D bent to E while sustaining the G for a wailing harmony bend, and G/C with the C hammered to D combined with lightning flashes down the scale to the A note. The effect is of a blast furnace door blowing wide open, but it is only prelude to measures 77–81 where he whips his strings with classic blues triplets of C pulled off to A, followed by E.

Intuitively realizing that a breather will only make his preceding virtuosic display of fretboard mastery even more powerful, Duane makes a horizontal foray down string 2 in measures 82–83 in order to cool off his tortured strings, back in the root position of the A Dorian mode where bends, sustained notes, and vibrato provide welcome contrast. A jaunt back up to the 12th position in measures 93–100 fools the listener into thinking Duane is going back up for another shot of high-register, high-energy riffing. However, by this point in his solo, he is entranced by his muse and is following wherever she may lead. Surprisingly, that becomes horizontally back down, up, down, and up on string 3 in A Dorian before making an abrupt relocation to the root position at fret 5 where he executes punchy quadruplets of E–G hammer-on/pull-offs that end on D in measures 104–107. Creating instantaneously now like a man possessed, Duane tap/trills at seemingly inhuman speed with the edge of his pick in measures 108–111 for textural contrast with a flashy technique that would even impress Eddie Van Halen.

In measures 113–120, he decides to repeat the harmony bends of measures 67–76 to whip up the musical tension again. He maintains the latest invention of tension in measures 121–124 with pull-offs from G to E at fret 12 that morphs into laser-like triplets of G–E–G. Harmonically, they relate consonantly to the i9 chord as the ♭7th and 5th and dissonantly to the IV6 as the 4th and 9th for an overall result of yet a different type of musical tension. The sizzling, sensational climax to his solo quickly ends with two prickly bends from G to the A over the IV6 and I, where the A functions as the 5th and the root for the long-awaited resolution, respectively. Not finished yet, Duane is joined by Dickey (Gtr. 2) in measures 125–128 for alternating unison riffs that could be seen to be derived from either the A Aeolian or Dorian modes, with the crucial addition of the hip, blues-approved ♭5th (E♭) that is emphasized with vibrato and produces anticipation and forward momentum.

Performance Tip: With the index finger anchored on the E note at fret 5 on string 2, tap hard and fast at frets 10 and 11 in measures 108–111. Be aware that playing a high-powered axe like a Les Paul through a flat-out Marshall helps to make the strings sensitive and receptive to such unorthodox techniques.

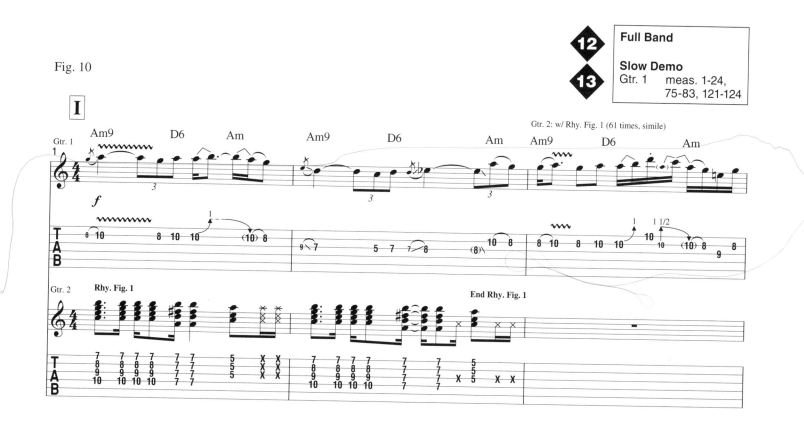

Fig. 10

In Memory of Elizabeth Reed

*Catch 2nd string
  under ring finger.

In Memory of Elizabeth Reed

*Played behind the beat.

**Played ahead of the beat.

***As before

In Memory of Elizabeth Reed

Pitch: E

In Memory of Elizabeth Reed

*Played behind the beat.

**Played ahead of the beat.

***Tap w/ edge of pick.

†Switch to bridge pickup.

*Played ahead of the beat.

In Memory of Elizabeth Reed

IT'S NOT MY CROSS TO BEAR

(*The Allman Brothers Band*, 1969)
Words and Music by Gregg Allman

Purportedly written by Gregg about the same former girlfriend as "Black Hearted Woman," "It's Not My Cross to Bear" was his second composition penned for the fledgling Allman Brothers Band after "Dreams." It is a dramatic, slow blues with jazzy changes that, as the second track on their debut album, announced to all the world that these southern "white boys" had the right to sing and play the blues with unapologetic authenticity and depth of expression.

Figure 11—Intro

Duane (Gtr. 1) ushers in this epochal blues landmark with the sweetest licks, creamiest tone, and washiest reverb this side of B.B. King playing the Regal Theater in 1964. The intro progression is eight sophisticated measures consisting of the same changes as the eight-measure verse: (I) B5–B5/A–B5/G♯–B5/F♯, B5–B5/A–B5/G♯–B5/F♯, (IV) E–E/D–E/C♯–E/B, and (iv) Em–Em/D–Em/C♯–Em/B; and a four-measure chorus (neither shown): (I) B, (vi) G♯m, (II7) C♯7, (V) F♯, (I) B5–B5/A–B5/G♯–B5/G, and (V) F♯. Utilizing the B minor pentatonic scale in the root and extension ("Albert King box") positions, along with the "B.B. King box" at fret 12, Duane makes a significant musical statement. Due to the rapidity of the chord changes, he takes the modal approach of alternating musical tension and resolution. A simple concept, it mainly consists of various bends for the former, while the root notes suffice for the latter. A cool exception occurs in measure 5 (I–vi), however, where he bends the 9th (C♯) to the major 3rd (D♯), followed by the sustained ♭3rd (D) to help define the quality of the chord changes.

Performance Tip: In measure 6, execute the quarter-step bends of the D and A notes with your index finger and play the B that follows with the ring finger.

Fig. 11

It's Not My Cross to Bear

Figure 12—Guitar Solo

After tastefully filling around Gregg's vocals with his instrumental "voice" in verses 1 and 2 (not shown), Duane steps back in for another eight-measure improvisational gem. Once again, he has at his disposal the root, extension, and B.B. King boxes of the B minor pentatonic scale, and, as in his intro solo, he is in no hurry because his phrases are as natural as breathing. For example, after making his entrance in measure 1 with a brief flurry of sixteenth notes using the 5th (F♯) and root (B) scale degrees, he rests before bending the ♭3rd (D) one half step to the major 3rd (D♯) to complement the I (B) chord tonality. After another graceful rest to start measure 2, Duane plays a pattern similar to measure 1 as a motif while slipping into the C♯ (9th, from the B Mixolydian mode) and bends up one step to the major 3rd as a hint of his soloing strategy to follow. Also, check out how he inserts the 6th (G♯) from the B Mixolydian mode to flesh out the B5/F♯ change.

In measures 3–4 of the IV (E) and iv (Em) chords, Duane creates subtle tension by repeatedly going to the 5th (B). He resolves it creatively and melodically, for instance, by playing the D against the E/D chord and the C♯ against the E/C♯ chord in measure 3. Beginning in measure 4 of the particularly dramatic E minor changes, he starts a spectacularly soulful, melodic, and sophisticated series of licks that run through the climactic conclusion in measure 8. After building musical tension in measure 4 again with mainly the 5th, he finally loosens the pressure by resolving to the root (E). However, continuing through to measure 5 of the I (B)–vi (G♯m) chord changes, respectively, Duane switches to the B major pentatonic scale played in the root position of G♯ minor pentatonic where it masquerades as the favored relative minor scale of melody-conscious blues guitarists.

The effect adds to the inherent drama of the progression as he works the B and C♯ notes melodically on string 3 to snake through the I, VI7, and II7 (C♯7sus4) chords in measures 5–6. It also sets up the sensational lick that connects beats 4–12 of measure 6 of the II7 and V (F♯) chords. Once again paying homage to B.B. King, Duane walks a chromatic run down string 1 in the "B.B. King box" at fret 12, connects it to a broken B triad of the D♯, B, and F♯ notes (functioning as the 6th, 4th, and root notes of F♯), and then ends on the vibratoed ♭7th (E) for a bluesy hue over the F♯. Not yet quitting his melodic quest, he ramps up to the 4th (B) over the V chord and continues emphasizing it in measure 7 of the I (B) chord. Instead of producing the expected resolution, though, it actually creates anticipation due to the descending, diatonic bass line under the B5 voicings. With unerring logic and supple phrasing, he resolves on the V chord of measure 15 by bending the ♭7th (E) to the root (F). Be aware that Dickey (Gtr. 2) takes the baton early in the relay from Duane in measure 8, and begins his jaunt (not shown) with a tart bend from the 5th (C♯) to the bluesy ♭6th (D) as a pickup into measure 9 and the next eight-measure progression.

Performance Tip: For the beautiful melodic phrase in measure 6, start with the middle finger on string 3 (G), followed by the ring (F♯), middle (F), and index (E and D) fingers. Slide with the index from the D to E, playing the B with the middle finger, and F♯ with the index. Complete the phrase by also playing the F and E with the index, adding B.B. King-like vibrato on the latter.

Fig. 12

Guitar Solo

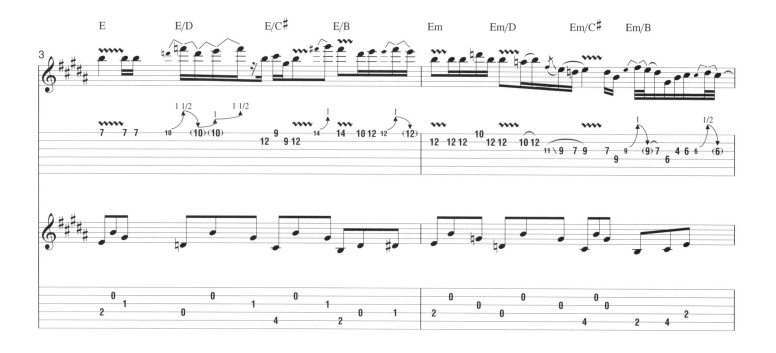

It's Not My Cross to Bear

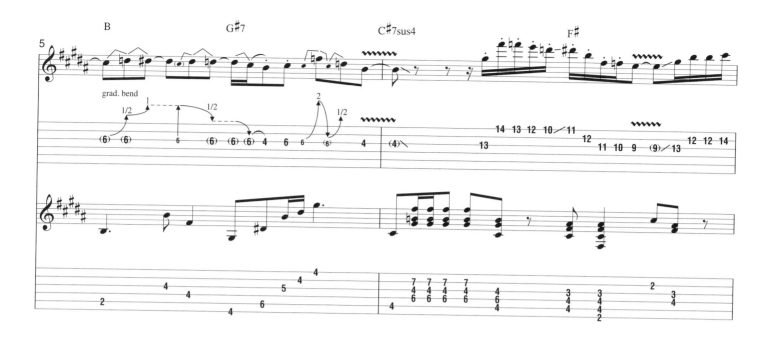

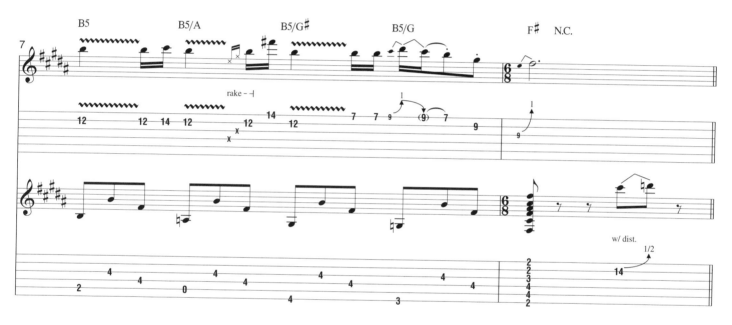

It's Not My Cross to Bear

LAYLA

(*Layla and Other Assorted Love Songs*, 1970)
Words and Music by Eric Clapton and Jim Gordon

A combination of his unbridled ambition and the recognition of his enormous talent following the release of the Allman's *Idlewild South* led Duane to accept Eric Clapton's invitation to play on the forthcoming Derek & the Dominos album. What was to be only one or two songs turned into most of the two-disc set, including the epic title track. Due to several factors, including lack of record company promotion, their decision to first release a severely edited single in 1970, and the fact that the public did not immediately realize that "Derek" was "Eric," it was not until after Duane's death that the full-length version became a #10 hit in 1972. It has since gone on to become Clapton's "theme song" and a heavily-requested rock-radio classic.

Figure 13—Intro

Apparently, Clapton had three verses written for "Layla" and told Duane he was still searching for a guitar hook to drive the song. He accepted the challenge and created one of rock's greatest riffs (Gtr. 3). Duane slyly constructed the bass lick from the vocal melody of the first line of Albert King's version of "As the Years Go Passing By," combined with the rock-approved D5, C5, and B♭5 power chords. The result is so distinctive, powerful, and complete that it could have functioned as a separate song all on its own.

Performance Tip: Use the middle finger to hammer-on and pull-off the fretted bass notes in the pickup and measure 2 of Gtr. 3. Play the D5, C5, and B♭5 chords in measures 1 and 2 with the index and ring fingers, low to high. For the G note on string 6 at fret 3, use the middle finger in measure 1 and the index finger in measure 2.

Fig. 13

Intro
Moderately ♩ = 116

*Duane Allman
**Original recording sounds 1/4 step sharp.

Figure 14—Guitar Solo

Duane cruises the sonic stratosphere, high above the surging rhythm of his bass string riff for his solo's 25 lyrical measures. In standard tuning, he uses a form of the D composite blues scale centered around the root (D), 2nd (E), ♭3rd (F), 4th (G), 5th (A), and ♭7th (C) notes, virtually all above fret 13, residing in the vicinity of the root-octave note at fret 22 on string 1 that he slides over repeatedly. On "top" of that, he frequently extends his slide with unerring accuracy past the end of the fingerboard of his 22-fret 1957 Gibson Les Paul Goldtop on string 1 to what would be frets 24 (E) and 25 (F) in measure 1, all the way up to "frets" 27 (G), 28 (G♯), 29 (A), and even 34 (D, two octaves above fret 10!) in measure 8.

Given the cyclical nature of the two measures that comprise Rhy. Fig. 1 with the tonality focused on the tonic (D) chord, by necessity, Duane takes a modal approach to his solo. Rather than playing licks that alternately create musical tension and release, as usually encountered in modal solos, he keeps the energy and intensity full-up the whole time. The most amazing aspect of this overwhelming virtuosic display is not just the exceptional technique, but the seemingly endless series of connected melodic ideas (and the majority in counterpoint) that Duane manages to squeeze out with his Coricidin bottle on strings 1 and 2. Many of them involve the root and ♭7th notes at frets 22 and 20, respectively, which produce a bluesy tinge even though the progression does not contain the typical I, IV, and V chords associated with the blues.

Performance Tip: The only way to become proficient at playing slide beyond the neck is to slowly and carefully practice nailing precise scale tones on the top two strings until you can recognize them by ear.

Fig. 14

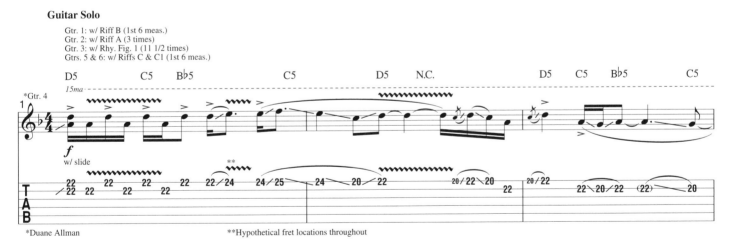

Layla

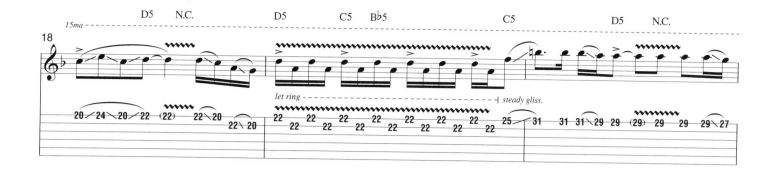

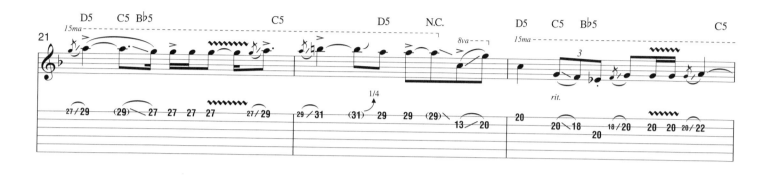

Slower ♩ = 109

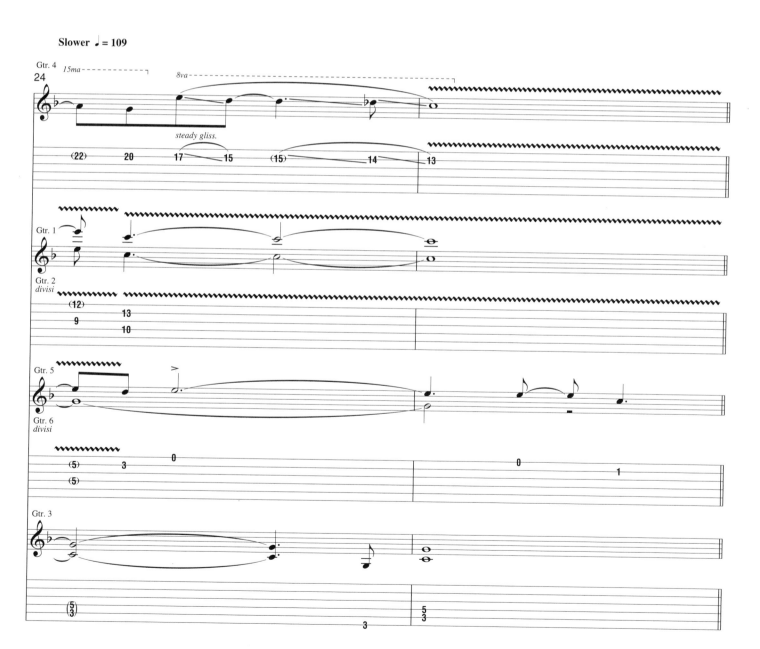

Layla

Figure 15—Outro

The interlude and outro were added last to the evolving opus of Eric Clapton's passionate love song to Pattie Boyd Harrison, the wife of Beatle George Harrison. Drummer Jim Gordon had been secretly recording his own material during the *Layla* sessions, but when by chance Clapton heard him play a piano piece he liked, he requested it for the outro of "Layla," so he and Duane played a dueling duet with their slides. Though somewhat similar in tone and style, Duane (Gtr. 4) and his fatter Les Paul stand out next to Clapton (Gtr. 2) and his leaner-sounding 1956 Stratocaster named "Brownie," that was famously featured in the album's back cover photo.

Figure 15 shows measures 1–24 (sections AAB of the 36-measure AABBC format) of the lengthy outro for a taste of Duane responding to a diatonic chord progression with a few substitutions, as opposed to the more typical I–IV R&B vamps or I–IV–V blues changes he was used to addressing. As the outro is in the key of C, he utilizes all the notes of the C major scale (*Ionian mode*, C–D–E–F–G–A–B). Observe, however, the exception in measure 22 where the D (II), instead of the diatonic Dm (ii) chord appears, compelling him to play F♯ (3rd) in order to emphasize the D major tonality thereby following the progression even more precisely at that juncture.

With virtually no deviation, Duane skillfully picks from the choice chord tones (root, 3rd, 5th, and 7th) relative to each change while phrasing complementary to the chord melody of Gtr. 7's part. Measures 2–6, to pick just five out of many, are excellent examples of his great work. In measure 2 of the I chord (C), he sustains the 5th (G) for easygoing musical tension then releases it in measure 3 of the I (Cmaj7/E), following a repeat of the 5th by resolving to the root (C) on beat 4. In measure 4, he slides on the consonant and sweet 6th (D) over the IV (Fadd9 and F) chord along with the hip major 7th (E) over the Fmaj7. Showing his boundless creativity in measure 5 of the IV (F6 and F) chords, Duane plays the 5th (C) and 3rd (A) notes to emphasize the tonality, while in measure 6 of the ♭VII (B♭7), he just sustains the all-important 3rd (D) to finish the job.

In retrospect, the decision to attach an entire instrumental section to "Layla" in addition to Duane's solo was a winner. Besides giving the "blues brothers" another welcome chance to indulge their obvious musical empathy, it also extended and figuratively amplified the bittersweet content of the lyrics.

Performance Tip: Damping is always one the most critical aspects of great slide technique. It is especially so in measure 7 of the ♭VII chord where Duane is playing a broken C/G (2nd inversion C major) triad at fret 17 interspersed with the 4th (F) note on string 2 at fret 18. It is paramount to avoid sounding like the entire C triad has moved up one half-step to C♯, so be sure to carefully (and quickly) drop the heel of your right hand on the strings following the G note, at fret 17 on string 4 on beat 3 of measure 7, before accessing the E and F notes on string 2 on beat 2.

Fig. 15

Outro

*Chord symbols reflect overall harmony.

Layla

Figure 16—Outro (Free Time)

The "bird chirp" that Duane (Gtr. 4) produces with his slider in the very last measure of the outro is as much a signature of the song as the intro's main riff. Observe how he leads up to it by playing the root (C) at fret 20 on string 1 in measure 1, followed by a gliss up and off in measure 2. On beat 3 of measure 3, he "chirps" like a "free bird" with the muted octave G note at fret 15 on string 1 and glisses down and off the string.

Performance Tip: Lightly mute string 1 with your right hand's heel and strike the note crisply. It helps to have "performance" level volume and a degree of distortion on the amp to achieve the desired effect.

Fig. 16

*Composite arrangement; Gtr. 8 (acous.)

Layla

LEAVE MY BLUES AT HOME

(*Idlewild South*, 1970)
Words and Music by Gregg Allman

Before it was named John F. Kennedy International Airport in 1963 in honor of the fallen president, the sprawling airport on Long Island near New York City was called Idlewild. A cabin in the woods near Macon that the "brothers" once rented was so busy with guests coming and going that they referred to it as "Idlewild South," hence the title of their second album. Considered by many to be their best studio work, it made a respectable showing at #38 on the pop charts. "Leave My Blues at Home" is the last track on the disc and sums up their evolution to date with funk, R&B, and blues elements.

Figure 17—Intro

Following four measures of Gregg's piano, Duane (Gtr. 1) and Dickey (Gtr. 2) combine to complete the stone-funk groove with four measures of a I-chord vamp (D9). Duane's years as an R&B session cat at Muscle Shoals studio serve him well as he spanks D9 1st-inversion (3rd on the bottom) voicings at fret 5. Observe the critical aspect of sliding into the chord, from either one fret below or above, to provide that "organic quality" inherent in blues-based music. Also, check out how Gtr. 2 features D major pentatonic licks voiced in the root position of the B minor pentatonic scale as another level of harmony and syncopation.

Performance Tip: Use the middle finger for the 3rd on string 4, and barre strings 3–1 with the ring finger.

Fig. 17

*Chord symbols reflect overall harmony.
***Dickey Betts

Figure 18—Interlude

Over a I-chord vamp (D7), Duane and Dickey create a three-part interlude that progresses from a harmonized, horn-like pattern in measures 1–2 that repeats four times, to a melodic, four-measure harmony line that builds into a five-measure call-and-response where they trade a combination of short licks that start out identical and evolve to similar variations. In measures 1–2, Duane takes the upper voice as they mostly play in bluesy 3rds. Be sure to see, however, that the dissonant chords on beats 3 and 4 of measure 2 are executed individually by Duane and Dickey, respectively. This is partially confirmed by G/C (4th/♭7th) on beat 3 being the cleaner-sounding guitar (Gtr. 2, panned right), and the woozy, triple-stop bend of E/A♯/F (9th/♯5th/♭3rd) by the more distorted axe (Gtr. 1, panned left) on beat 4.

In measures 3 and 4, Duane and Dickey take their signature twin-guitar harmony to a more exotic place with slightly dissonant 4ths that climb the fingerboard in the process of subtly kicking the intensity level up a notch at the peak of the interlude. Sweet, ringing, harmonious 6ths in measure 5 reverse the effect and lead to tightly focused octaves with less musical tension on the way to measures 7–11. There, Gtr. 1 and Gtr. 2 trade and intertwine short, gently flowing licks from several positions of the D minor pentatonic scale with an added 9th (E). Check out how Dickey plays the exact same three licks in measures 7–8 that end on the 5th (A) for musical tension, and then a different pair in measures 10–11 that resolve to the root (D). Meanwhile, Duane first mimics Dickey in measure 7 before breaking away with improvised variations that give a spacious, airy feel to the proceedings following the tight, taut structures that preceded them. The result facilitates a smooth transition to the percussion breakdown (not shown) that follows by winding down the action in advance.

Performance Tip: Use the strong index, middle, and ring fingers on strings 3–1, respectively, to bend the double stop on beat 4 of measure 2.

Fig. 18

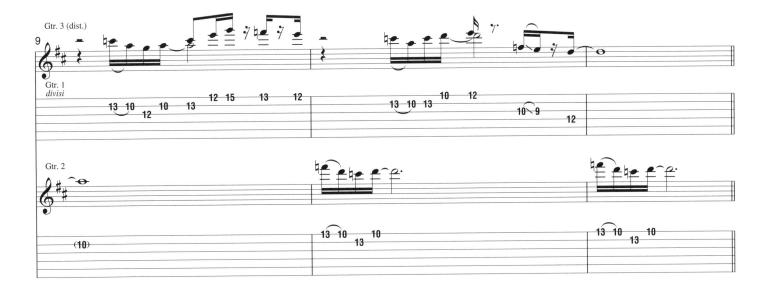

Figure 19—Outro Guitar Solo

For 19 measures up to the fade, Duane (Gtr. 3) and Dickey (Gtr. 4) "duke it out" over the I-chord vamp (D9) from the verse with the D composite blues scale. Rare in an ABB studio recording, this exchange clearly illuminates their differences and similarities as exceptional lead guitarists. Keith Richards and Ron Wood, among other famous guitar tandems in rock music, may often be analyzed the same way.

Be aware that Dickey is panned left and Duane is to the right of the mix. It is Dickey who fires the first volley in measures 1–2 where they trade off every two measures in sync with the two-measure vamp of Figs. 1 & 1A. Both guitarists have *beaucoup* chops and phrase with fluidity and a supreme sense of swing. However, it can be seen in the outro that Duane, who Dickey has described as the generally more aggressive and fiery between them, tends to repeat notes and licks more often to produce his combustible musical tension; measures 3, 11, 15, 16, and 19 bear this out. Dickey, on the other hand, is more likely to dynamically ascend and descend the scale as heard in measures 1, 2, and 5. However, there are also those instances where they do just the opposite. In measure 4, Duane gracefully descends the scale, while Dickey vigorously repeats a bend from the 2nd (E) to the tonality-defining major 3rd (F♯) in measures 13–14. Notice that both Duane and Dickey tend to make the last note in each of their two-measure phrases either the root (D) or 5th (A). Though their choice is likely based on instinct and intuition of the moment, the effect is to create resolution with the root and moderate musical tension with the 5th, which is the hallmark of modal soloing.

Performance Tip: In measure 15, bend the 9th (E) at fret 12 on string 1 with the ring finger and use the index finger for the 5th (A) on string 2 at fret 10.

Fig. 19

Outro Guitar Solo

Gtrs. 1 & 2: w/ Rhy. Figs. 1 & 1A (9 1/2 times)

*Dickey Betts   **Duane Allman

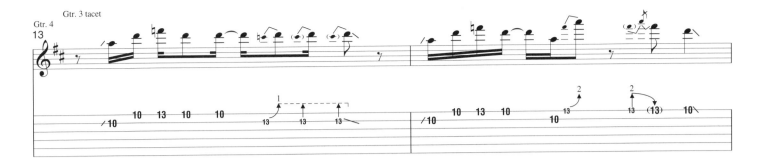

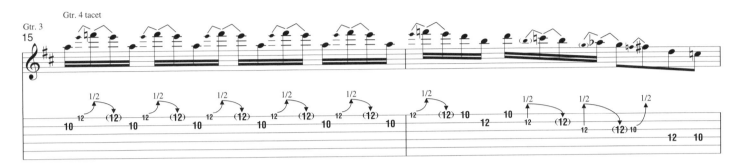

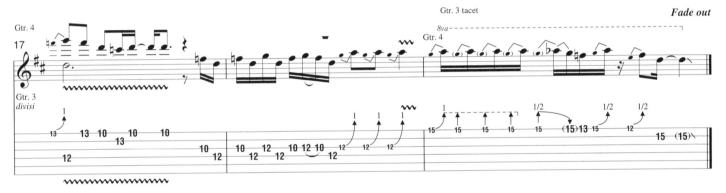

LITTLE MARTHA

(*Eat a Peach*, 1972)
Written by Duane Allman

As the only ABB composition credited solely to Duane, it also features him playing his 1937–39 National Duolian. The short instrumental was written in honor of a girlfriend named Dixie Lee Meadows, known to the band as one of the "Hot 'Lanta Girls," but whom Duane affectionately called "Little Martha." No less a fingerstyle master than Leo Kottke referred to the song as "one of his ABB favorites" and he recorded a version on *Shout Towards Noon* in 1986. On the original vinyl double album, the elegiac composition closed side 3 elegantly and eloquently.

Figure 20—Section B (Theme)

Duane (Gtr. 1) and Dickey (Gtr. 2) are both tuned to open E, a tuning long favored by blues slide guitarists who are also drawn to open D. The latter is the same relative tuning except that strings are detuned, for less tension on the neck, rather than tuned up as in open E. Duane and Dickey perform as a duo throughout, though Duane carries the bulk of the musical weight and could have actually performed the tune solo as Kottke later did. The eight-measure theme (including measure 8 in 5/4 time) contains I (E), IV (A), and V (B) changes, but is not in a traditional blues format. Rather, it is a gentle, wistful folk instrumental in the tradition of Kottke, John Fahey, and other masters of American steel-string fingerstyle music.

Performance Tip: Use the right-hand thumb, index, and middle fingers for the most efficient fingerstyle approach. The thumb will handle strings 6 and 5; the index, strings 4 and 3; and the ring, strings 2 and 1. Barre strings 4–1 at fret 5 with the index finger for the IV (A) change in measure 5.

Fig. 20

25 Full Band

26 Slow Demo
Gtr. 1   meas. 1-4

Figure 21—Section C (Bridge)

The eight-measure bridge provides a release from the theme by creating musical tension that is not conclusively resolved back to the tonic (E) chord until the last measure. Also, where the theme has a consistently driving rhythm, the bridge contains syncopated chord accents that contribute a sense that the time is being dynamically suspended. Observe how the bridge is divided into four, one-measure phrases. Measure 1 moves vi–IV–V–V (C#m/B–A/B–B). Measure 2 contains vi–IV–V7 (B7) changes. Measure 3 is the same as 1, but measure 4 functions as a turnaround with I–V7–I chords for a hint of the blues that coursed through Duane's body and bloodstream.

27	Full Band
28	Slow Demo
	Gtr. 1 meas. 1-4
	Gtr. 2 meas. 1-4

Fig. 21

MOUNTAIN JAM

(*Eat a Peach*, 1972)
Words and Music by Donovan Leitch, Duane Allman, Gregg Allman, Dickey Betts, Berry Oakley, Jaimoe Johanny Johanson and Butch Trucks

Originally recorded at the famous Fillmore East concerts in the spring of 1971, the epic 33-minute long "Mountain Jam" was too lengthy to include on *Live at Fillmore East*. Under deadline to finish their third "studio" album with scant new material, however, Gregg and Dickey decided to put the entire song on the album as a tribute to Duane, while also extending the new release into a hit double-disc set.

Figure 22—Section A

Duane (Gtr. 1) segues into "Mountain Jam" from his cadenza at the end of the coda of "Whipping Post" while barely pausing for a breath. Over a I-chord vamp (E) he utilizes the root position of the E major pentatonic scale, voiced as the C♯ minor hexatonic scale, and improvises around the original Donovan vocal melody as Dickey (Gtr. 2) joins the fun. For 48 measures, they lightly spar and intertwine until joining for a harmonized interpretation of sections B and C (not shown).

The one-step bend of the 2nd (F♯) to the major 3rd (G♯) on string 3 at fret 11 is a typical move in the scale and Duane employs it right off in measure 2 for part of the melody and throughout as a motif. Likewise, short, concise licks featuring regular resolution to the root (E) on string 3 at fret 9 occur as typical in the modal solo. However, in measures 15–17 and 29–32, Duane indulges his whimsy in longer, lyrical runs up and down the scale that include the 4th (A) on string 2 at fret 10 for melodic purposes and more importantly, as an excellent way to create musical tension that naturally resolves to the 3rd (G♯) on string 2 at fret 9.

Performance Tip: The index finger should be used to play all notes on all strings at fret 9.

Fig. 22

*Key signature denotes E Mixolydian.
***Dickey Betts

Figure 23—Section F (Guitar Solo 1)

After the harmonizing melody lines with Dickey, Duane takes the first solo in 70 exemplary measures over the same I-chord vamp (E). As the goal of any modal solo is to create a smooth flow of notes and licks producing musical tension and release, he shows off an astonishing variety of means. One of his immediate choices is the emphasis of the ♭9th (F) on string 2 at fret 6 as an extremely brash note in measures 17–20. The first time it is heard in measure 17 and sustained in measure 18, it is so dissonant that it almost sounds like a mistake. By the time it quickly appears again in measure 19 and is sustained into measure 20, it begins to sound hip with its Middle Eastern flavor. Observe that Duane refuses to take the cheap way out and follow right up by resolving it to the root (E). Instead, he keeps the energy and anticipation goosed up with longer melodic runs (including the F again) until reaching the root in measure 28.

Beginning in measure 48 through to measure 52, he decides to turn up the juice with his phrasing in order to power up the tension. He uses a series of rapidly repeating sixteenth-note quadruplets that dynamically, rhythmically, and harmonically contrast with the vamp. In measure 48, he alternates two riffs: the first one contains the root (E) on string 1 at fret 12 pulled off to the 6th (C♯) followed by the root on string 3 at fret 9, while the variation has the 5th (B) on string 2 at fret 12 pulled off to the 3rd (G♯) followed by the root on string 3. In measure 49, he just repeats the second riff. In measure 50, the combination of the 4th (A), 2nd (F♯), and ♭7th (D) produces harmonic tension and a hint of dominant tonality over the vamp's tonic triad that is released in measure 51 when Duane repeats the riff from measure 49. Capping the breathless onrush of notes are the patterns in measure 52, where Duane chromatically climbs from the 2nd (F♯) to the 3rd (G♯) as he pulls off to the root then picks the 5th (B). It is a true-fire climactic method of moving away from repeating riffs to combine with the one-step bends of the ♭3rd to the 4th (A) on beats 3 and 4 and on to measure 53. Check out how he then skillfully slows the momentum in measure 53 with a half-step bend of the ♭3rd to the major 3rd (G) followed by a sustained E/B double stop (root/5th) for resolution on beat 4 of measure 53.

Duane has one more slick trick to trot out as he employs chiming harmonics in measures 61–68 before settling back down to his (occasional) role of rhythm guitarist in measures 69–71 to ease into Gregg's organ solo (not shown). However, his entrance into this concluding section of the solo is unusual and highly creative as he first executes a funky country-blues quarter-step bend from the ♭3rd (G) to the "true blue note," then a half-step on string 6 at fret 3, followed by the open 6th string (E). Allowing the open-E string to sustain underneath, Duane then plucks the harmonics of E and B at fret 12 on strings 1 and 2 over the top of measures 61–63. In measures 65–66, he plays a melodic "string" of harmonics with A, F♯, and D at fret 7 followed by the E on string 1, climaxing by "tremolo-ing" the E harmonic with his volume knob in measures 67–68.

Performance Tip: Harmonics are a "feel" thing. Using the flat part of the index finger above the first knuckle (as opposed to the tip of the index finger), lightly touch the string directly over the fret wire, lifting it off the string a fraction of a second after picking it. With a little practice, it will be possible to produce bell-like tones that sustain a significant length of time in conjunction with the characteristics of the guitar and amp.

Fig. 23

*Chord symbols reflect basic harmony.

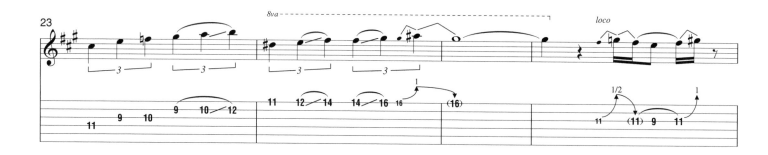

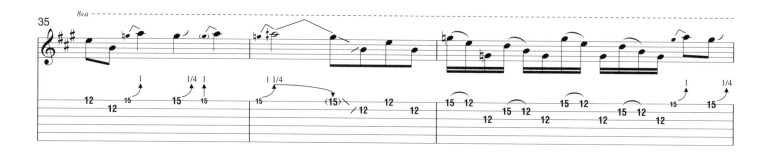

Mountain Jam

*Played behind the beat.

**Applies to
  harmonics only

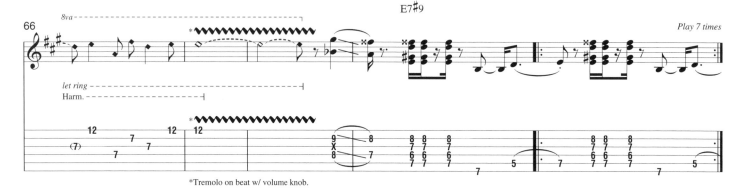

*Tremolo on beat w/ volume knob.

Figure 24—Section L (Guitar Solo 2)

Slipping behind Dickey in his solo, Duane (Gtr. 1) places the Coricidin bottle on his ring finger to slither over the I (E), I, ♭VII (D), and v7 (Bm7) changes with major and minor triads, and provides a big "pad" for his guitar partner. Dig how he utilizes F♯/D/A at fret 7 to imply both D major (3rd/root/5th) and Bm7 (5th/♭3rd/♭7th).

Dickey passes the figurative baton in measure 16, and Duane goes on to solo with great verve and inventiveness, in standard tuning, to measure 87, where he removes his slider to continue soloing at Section M (not shown). Check out that Dickey duets with Duane to measure 31.

The change in sound with the slide is striking, dynamic, and exhilarating, and only serves to further confirm the epic masterpiece of improvisation that is "Mountain Jam." Beginning in measure 33, Duane parlays the classic dyad of E/B (root/5th) at fret 12 into a jumping-off point to sometimes follow the chord changes, where he starts with the 4th (A) for tension, and nips the 3rd (G♯) and 5th (B) to imply an E major tonality. In measure 48 (played 5 times), he sings the whistling double-octave E/B for tension at what would be fret 24 (past the end of the fingerboard on most guitars) as the chords cycle through accented I (E), I, ♭VII (D)–v7 (Bm7), and v7–♭VII changes. He continues the dyad into measure 49 where he zooms up even higher to what would be fret 27 for a searing ♭3rd (G), repeating it in measure 49 as tension peaks.

In measures 50–58, Duane presents a rich selection of notes over each change that is at once logical and harmonious and contributes to the forward momentum of the song at that point. Using the E composite blues scale in the root position around fret 12, he descends and ascends the scale with his customary fluidity. The end result is that it connects him smoothly to measures 59–61, where he briefly joins the rhythm section to play dyads and triads indicating the I (E) and ♭VII (D) chords, before lyrically soaring on string 1 above fret 12 in measures 63–66 for one of his signature forays. Over the I chord in measures 64–65, Duane wiggles back and forth between the 4th (A) and major 3rd (G♯) at frets 17 and 16, respectively. Over the ♭VII change in measure 66 he mainly emphasizes the 5th (A). Observe, however, how he begins to descend on beats 3 and 4 with the ♭5th (F) at fret 16 on the way to the 5th (F♯) of the v7 chord in measure 67, which descends to the 4th (E) that functions as the root for resolution on the I chord of measure 68.

Duane displays his ear for composition on the way to completing his excellent adventure with the slide; this occurs starting in measures 74 and 75 of the ♭VII (D) and v7 (Bm7) changes where he plays just the 3rd (F♯) and root (B) notes, respectively, in rippling triplets, before sustaining the 5th (B) over the I chord in measures 76–77. In measures 76–79 of the ♭VII chord, he repeats the 3rd and then moves to the jazzy major 7th (D♯), also in triplets, before sustaining the 5th over the I chord in measures 80–81. Finally, in measures 82–83 of the ♭VII chord, he once again repeats the 3rd with triplets to confirm the major tonality, but follows up with a run down the D major scale (with the inclusion of the snarky ♭5th) on the way to the 5th (B) over the I chord in measures 84–85 to keep the tension percolating along. A section of elastic glisses and random instrumental effects then commence as Duane allows his slide solo to "deconstruct," as dynamic contrast to the brilliantly controlled sonic excitement that preceded it, on the way to picking up the action for yet another extended fret ride, sans Coricidin bottle, at Section M.

Performance Tip: Pluck the notes of the triads in measure 62 simultaneously with the thumb, index, and middle fingers (low to high, respectively).

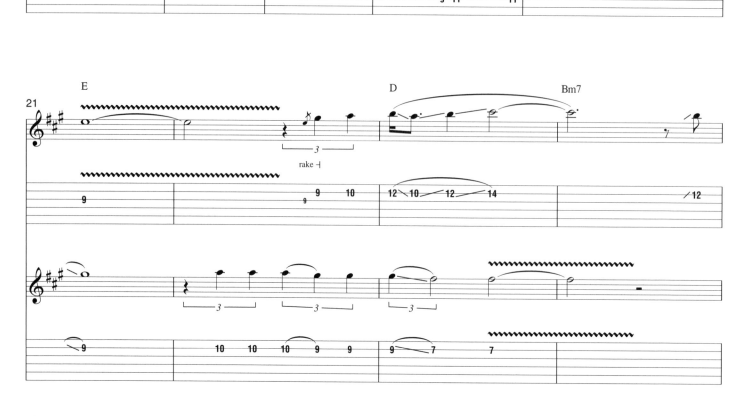

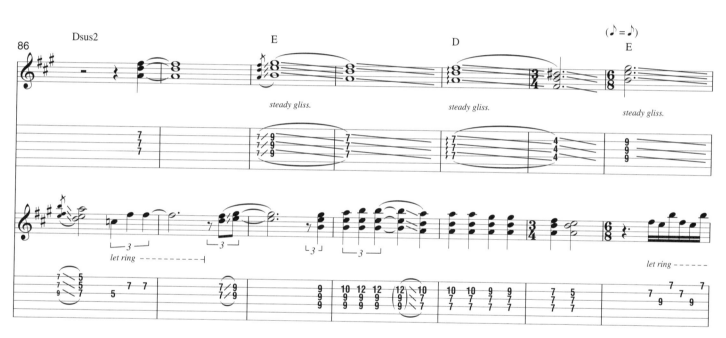

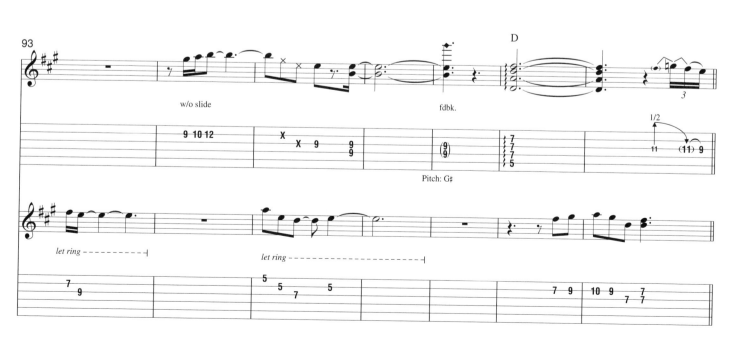

Mountain Jam

(THEY CALL IT) STORMY MONDAY (STORMY MONDAY BLUES)

(*At Fillmore East*, 1971)
Words and Music by Aaron "T-Bone" Walker

The ABB version of T-Bone Walker's "Stormy Monday" is based most prominently on the hit 1961 recording by Bobby "Blue" Bland with guitarist Wayne Bennett—hence Gregg referring to it as an "old Bobby Bland song" in his spoken intro, before correcting himself. Like their take on "One Way Out" and "You Don't Love Me," it has become the gold standard for succeeding generations of young blues musicians.

Figure 25—Intro

Duane (Gtr. 1) brings in this slow blues showcase all by himself with two measures in the style of T-Bone Walker, by employing the "Father of Electric Blues"-patented, moveable *1st-inversion* (3rd on bottom) 9th chords, with the addition of a D(♯5) nicked from Bland's version, instead of the more common D7 chord, for the V chord in measure 3.

In the 12-bar chorus of instrumental blues that follows, he plays sliding 6ths relative to the I9 (G9) and IV9 (C9) changes in measures 3–8, implying 6/9 chords that are prime signature licks from the accompaniment of "Stormy Monday." Measures 9–10 that usually contain the I chord instead have jazzy substitutions of I7 (G7)–ii7 (Am7) and iii7 (Bm7)–♭iii7 (B♭m7), also, as in the Bland version, voiced as full, six- and five-string barre chords. Measures 11–12 that generally have the V and IV changes feature ii7 (Am7) and iv (Cm)–iv7 (Cm7) instead. In measures 13–14 of the turnaround, Duane arranges partial G9 chords, sliding 6ths, and the arpeggiated D(♯5) voicing into a smooth and full accompaniment that could have sufficed on its own without the expert chording of Dickey (Gtr.2).

Performance Tip: For the D(♯5) chord, barre with the index finger at fret 3 on strings 3 and 2 using the ring finger on string 5 and the middle finger on string 4.

Fig. 25

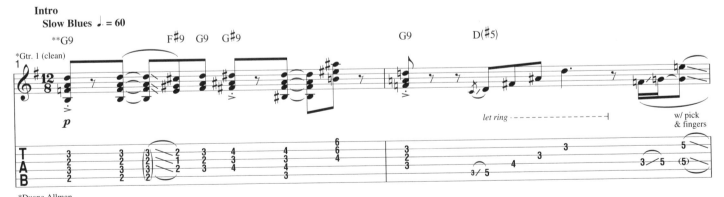

*Duane Allman
**Chord symbols reflect overall harmony.

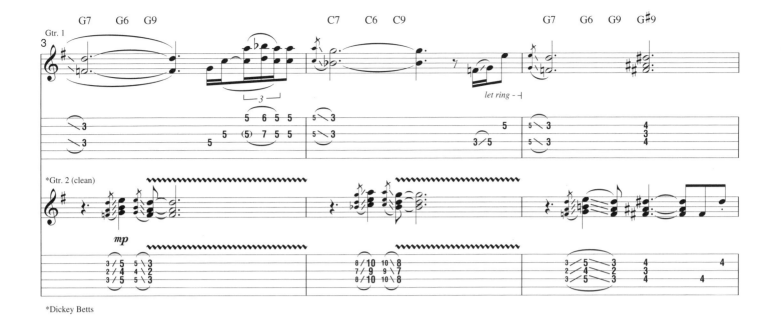

*Dickey Betts

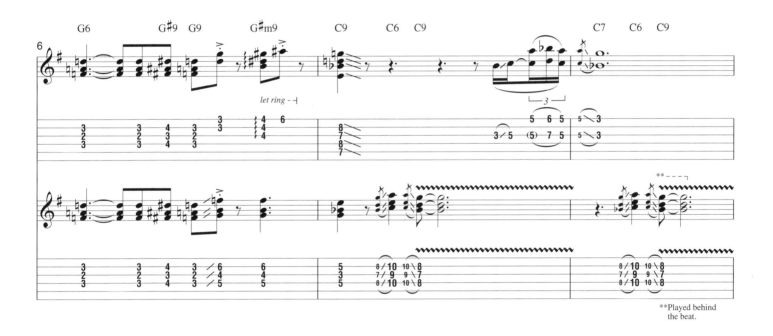

**Played behind
the beat.

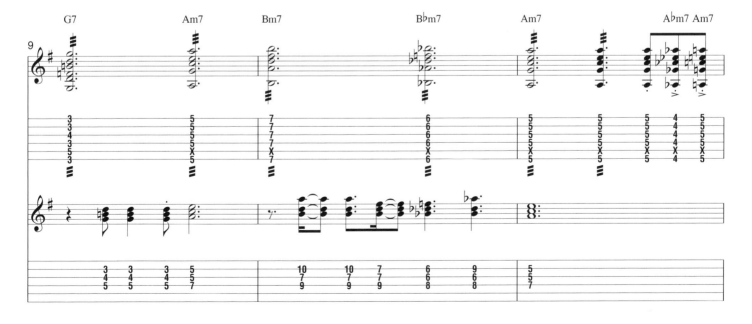

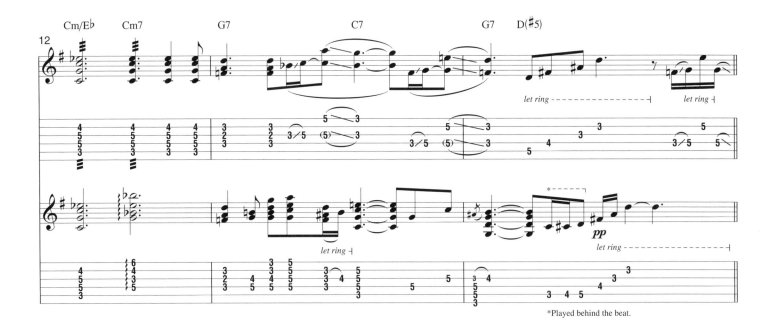

*Played behind the beat.

Figure 26—Guitar Solo

Eric Clapton was quoted as saying that Duane's playing on Wilson Pickett's version of "Hey Jude" scared him. If anything could have and should have done it, however, it is Duane's flawless, fluid, melodic, and downright devastating solo on "Stormy Monday." Through two passionate 12-bar choruses, he combines intelligent note selection, consisting of chord tones and hip scale degrees like a jazz man, along with deeply expressive phrasing as expected from a master bluesman. Not coincidentally, his naturally-distorted sound has the robust overtones and brilliant harmonics of a horn.

In measures 1–4 of the I7 (G7), IV9 (C9), and I7 changes, Duane adopts his B.B. King persona and parks his Les Paul in the "B.B. King box" around fret 8, where he utilizes the G composite blues scale to great advantage. In measure 1, he bends the 9th (A) to the 3rd (B) to emphasize the G major tonality. In measure 2, he pays direct homage to the once and future "King" on beats 3 and 4 by bending into the 3rd (E) followed by the 5th (G), 6th (A), and 5th of IV9. Duane then cleverly manipulates the same basic compact group of notes in measures 3–4 of the I7 change to do his bidding. He firmly establishes the tonality by again bending the 9th (A) to the 3rd (B) followed by the root (G) in measure 3. Musical tension is then created in measure 4 with the 5th (D) bent one step to the sweet 6th (E), and the 9th bent a bluesy half step to the nasty ♭3rd (B♭), before he resolves to the root (G) with slinky vibrato.

By repeating the G note (now functioning as the 5th of C) on string 2 at fret 8, Duane makes a seamless move down the fingerboard to the extension position of the G minor pentatonic scale, also known as the "Albert King box," over the IV9 change in measures 5–6. He creates more tension in measure 5 by first bending the 4th (F) a half step to the blues-approved ♭5th (F♯) and then sends it up in pitch to the ♭7th (B♭) to confirm the C dominant tonality. In measure 6, he becomes even more daring with a two-step bend from the 5th to the decidedly non-bluesy major 7th (B) on beat 3. But this is all prelude for what is to follow after he completes his journey down the fingerboard by relocating to the root position of the G minor pentatonic scale on beat 4, with a classic lick that ends on the 5th to maintain anticipation into the next critical section of the progression.

Having planned ahead, Duane is now ready to follow the ascending chord substitutions in measures 7–8 of the I chord with his own ascension through the scale positions up the neck. Check out how he moves in harmonious sync with the I7 (G7), ii (Am), and iii (Bm) changes by emphasizing the 3rd (B), root (A), and root (B) notes. When he gets

(They Call It) Stormy Monday (Stormy Monday Blues)

to the $\flat$iii (B$\flat$m) and $\flat$iii7 (B$\flat$m7) changes in measure 8, however, he resorts back to the tonic note of G that functions as the 6th for musical tension. He smartly refuses to stop the forward momentum of his solo by going directly to the root (A) of the ii chord in measure 9. Instead, he bends the root one-half step to the hot $\flat$9th (B$\flat$) and releases it for an eighth note, followed by a one-step bend from the 9th (B) to the very dissonant major 3rd (C$\sharp$), and lastly another one-step bend to the 9th. In measure 10 of the iv (Cm/E$\flat$) and iv7 (Cm7) chords, Duane creates a whole world of melody, harmony, and rubbery bending by first establishing resolution with the $\flat$7th (B$\flat$) bent one step to the root (C) followed by the 5th (G). The half-step bend from the 4th (F) to the gritty $\flat$5th (F$\sharp$), before moving nicely to the $\flat$7th (B$\flat$) of Cm7 on beat 3, is followed by a stunning lick on beat 4 of the $\sharp$5th (G$\sharp$) and $\flat$3rd (E$\flat$) with harmonics resolving to the root note.

The turnaround in measures 11 and 12 is a wonder of inventiveness and spontaneity that keeps attention riveted to see what Duane will do next. Every beat tells a story: on beat 1, he executes a classic blues bend from the $\flat$3rd (B$\flat$) of the I (G) chord to the "true blue note" in between the $\flat$3rd and major 3rd (B) before resolving to the root (G). On beat 2, he glisses dramatically from G/D (root/5th) at fret 3 to the octave at fret 15. On beat 3, he vibratos the 5th (G) of the IV (C) chord at fret 15, followed by a keening, shimmering unison bend on beat 4 of the same note to intensify the musical tension. In measure 12 on beats 1 and 2, he returns "home" to the B.B. King box via the 6th (E) and root (G) notes. He then uses the root (G) as a target note, complemented by the 3rd (B bent to A), and surrounded by tension notes of the 9th (A) and $\flat$9th (A$\flat$). On beat 3, he vibratos the root of the V (D[$\sharp$5]) chord before launching a preemptive strike on his second 12-bar chorus by again sliding into the E, followed by the G in the B.B. King box on beat 4.

Duane sets the scene for measure 1 of the I7 chord with the 5th (D) on string 1 at fret 10 as a source for the majority of licks. After bending it one step to the 6th (E), he briefly touches on the 3rd (B) at fret 7, before repeating the one-step bend that is followed by a 1-1/2 step bend to the $\flat$7th (F) that nails the G7 tonality. He sails back down to the IV7 (C7) chord by re-bending to the 6th and ending on the 5th to keep the tension afloat. In measure 14, he adjourns to the B.B. King box again and establishes the C7 tonality with the 6th (A) bent one-half step to the $\flat$7th (B$\flat$), followed by the 5th (G), 3rd (E), and $\flat$7th. Observe how he repeats the major 3rd of C to conclusively project the critical change to the IV chord from the I chord. In measures 15–16 of the I7 chord, he resorts back to the 5th (D) on string 1, going so far as to virtually repeat the licks from measure 13 as a motif. In measure 16, he makes his guitar sing with righteous abandon via a series of alternating one and 1-1/2-step bends from the 5th that produces startling musical tension.

For measures 17–18 of the IV7 (C7) change, Duane once again returns to the B.B. King box that is so effective at indicating the IV chord tonality through easy access to the crucial 3rd (E), 5th (G), and $\flat$7th (B$\flat$). Numerous varied and fluid bends with fat vibrato on the repeating 5th create a rich tapestry of blues power as anticipation and preview to his second journey up the ascending chord substitutions awaiting his attention, and our listening pleasure, in measures 19 and 20. As in measures 7–8 of his first chorus of blues, Duane selects the 3rd (B) over the I (G) chord, though this time he is an octave higher and bends the 9th (A) up one step to access it. Instead of playing the root (A) over the ii (Am), he bends the $\flat$9th (B$\flat$) to the tonality-defining $\flat$3rd (C), followed by the $\flat$7th (G) over the ii7 (Am7) change. Though he briefly picks the root (B) over the iii (Bm) in measure 20 before bending it one step to the 9th (C), he executes a soaring bend of 1-1/2 steps to the $\flat$3rd (D) over the iii7 (Bm7), while ending the measure with the 6th (G) over the $\flat$iii7 (B$\flat$m7) and $\flat$iii (B$\flat$m) changes. The result is a memorable smorgasbord of melody, harmony, and bluesy spunk.

Duane commands his axe to "squawk" in measures 21–22 of the ii (Am) and iv (Cm/E$\flat$)–iv7 (Cm7/B$\flat$) chords, respectively, with another series of stuttering bends as a motif based on the A note functioning as the root of Am and the 6th of Cm. In measure 21, that is accomplished, similar to measure 16, by alternating between the root and a half-step bend to the ♭9th (B♭). In measure 10, Duane continues with the alternation on beat 1, but then begins winding the tension down as he heads toward the turnaround in measures 23–24. Starting with the 5th (G) on beat 2, he descends to the 4th (F) and root (C) for a brief resolution, before pulling a half-step bend from the ♭7th (B♭) to the major 7th (B) on beat 4; this resolves in the classic blues manner to the vibratoed tonic (G) in the root position of the G minor pentatonic scale on beat 1 of measure 24. Wishing to maintain a high level of intensity and to likewise climax his solo with sonic fireworks, Duane quickly relocates to the root-octave position of the composite blues scale at fret 15. In measure 23, rather than specifically target the I (G) and IV (C) chords, he keeps the focus on the G note, functioning as the root and 5th, respectively, by nicking it straight on and bending up to it from the F (♭7th or 4th, respectively). In measure 24 of the I chord, however, he descends, as another motif, from the ♭7th (F) bent 1-1/4 steps to the root, a half step to the major 7th (F♯), and from the 6th (E) bent to the major 7th before repeating the root (D) note of the D(♯5) chord on beats 3 and 4 for a satisfying resolution.

Performance Tip: Bend the ♭7th (B♭) on string 3, fret 3, beat 4 of measure 22 with the index finger by pulling down. Play the root note that follows on beat 1 of measure 23 with the middle finger, adding vibrato by pushing upwards.

Full Band

Slow Demo
Gtr. 1   meas. 11-24

Fig. 26

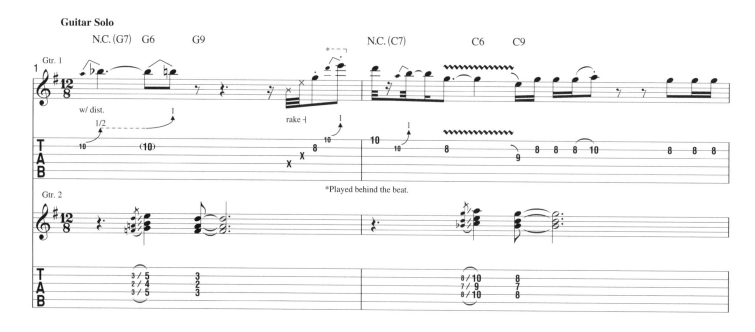

(They Call It) Stormy Monday (Stormy Monday Blues)

*Played behind the beat.

**Played ahead of the beat.

(They Call It) Stormy Monday (Stormy Monday Blues)

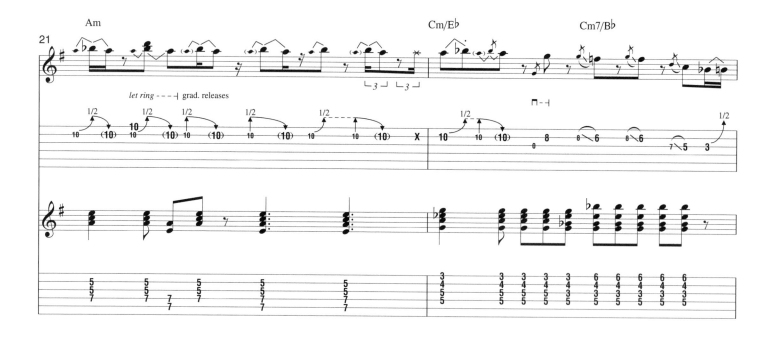

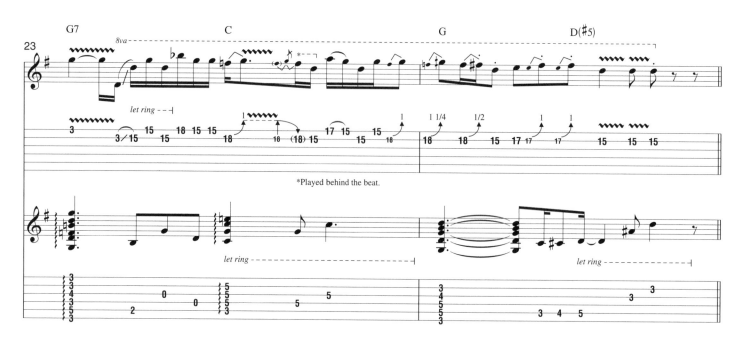

(They Call It) Stormy Monday (Stormy Monday Blues)

TROUBLE NO MORE (SOMEDAY BABY)

(The Allman Brothers Band, 1969)
Written by McKinley Morganfield (Muddy Waters)

This Muddy Waters classic was the song Duane picked for Gregg to "audition" with on March 26, 1969 in Jacksonville, Florida, for the soon-to-be formed Allman Brothers Band. It is one of the few songs on the debut album to feature both Butch Trucks and Jai Johanny "Jaimoe" Johnson playing on their full drum kits, simultaneously. On the original vinyl album, it closes side A as the first song to spring Duane playing slide on an unsuspecting audience that would come to adore him.

Figure 27—Intro

The eight-measure intro consists of a two-measure riff played four times. Duane (Gtr. 1), in standard tuning, plays one octave higher in sync with the acoustic guitar of Gtr. 3. Dickey on electric (Gtr. 2) also plays an almost identical pattern, but bends the ♭3rd (B♭) a quarter step to the "true blue note" in between the ♭3rd and major 3rd (B), while muting the root (G) on beat 4 of measures 1, 3, 5, and 7. Notice how Duane tends to move horizontally through several positions of the A minor pentatonic scale, rather than more vertically as Dickey does through two positions. This approach for playing slide in standard tuning is highly recommended as it minimizes the possibility of accidentally including unwanted dissonances from occurring on adjacent strings.

Performance Tip: Left- and right-hand muting is critical when playing slide under all circumstances; this is especially so in measures 1, 3, 5, and 7 when Duane moves between the G note on string 3 and the A and C notes, respectively, on string 2. Be sure to quickly mute the G with the right-hand thumb after plucking, then use the index finger for the A and C notes.

Fig. 27

Intro
Moderately fast ♩ = 138

*Gtr. 1 (elec.)

*Duane Allman
†Slide positioned halfway between 13th & 14th frets.

***Gtr. 2 (elec.)

***Dickey Betts
Gtr. 3 (acous.)

**Key signature denotes A Dorian.

1. Don't care how long you

Figure 28—Guitar Solo

Duane (Gtr. 1) comes on in his solo like gangbusters with a huge sound and utter confidence in his abilities. The 23 measures consist of 15 measures of the verse chords, plus nine additional measures of I (A), I, ♭III (C), ♭III, IV (D), IV, plus three measures of the V chord (E7♯9). Check out how the shapes for the I and IV chords are reminiscent of both "Green Onions" and "Help Me" by Sonny Boy Williamson with their A5–C5–D5 and D5–F5–G5 changes per measure, respectively.

Measures 8–12 contain an unusual 5 measures of the I chord as Duane "plays the changes" with precision and efficiency. In measures 2–5 he involves the root (A), 3rd (C♯), and 5th (E) degrees of the A major triad with the ♭3rd (C) and 4th (D) to form the A composite blues scale for a down-home taste of bluesy "grits." Equally important as his note selection, however, is his vocal-like phrasing that is as slippery as a Mississippi catfish and juicy as a Georgia peach by way of Chicago. In measures 6–7 of the IV chord, he creates "electric" musical tension by entering with the ♭7th (C) leading tone, to "lead" the ear into the change, and the 9th (E), while deliberately avoiding the root (D) but leaning heavily on the 5th (A).

Measures 8–12 of the I chord are similar to measures 2–5 with a noticeable change of phrasing and focus. He relentlessly blisters the root (A) note on string 3 at fret 14, coming at it from a variety of other scale tones, and using the sheer repetition to create tension and anticipation. In measures 13–16, Duane "slides" right along with Gtrs. 2 & 3 into the signature riff (Riffs A and A1, respectively) from the intro in an intelligent compositional move that smoothly transitions into a call-and-response section with Dickey for measures 17–24. Observe how Duane plays just C♯ and E, functioning as the 3rds of the A and C chords, respectively, to support the major tonality in measures 17–20, as he bides his time waiting to "respond" to the fluid and lyrical "call" of his guitar partner; when he does in measures 21–22, it is with a razor-sharp run over the IV chord utilizing the D composite blues scale with an inclusion of the major 7th (C♯), from the D major scale (Ionian mode) on beats 3 and 4 of measure 21, for a sweet bit of diatonic harmony that adds to the brilliance of the melody. In measure 22, Duane caps his exuberant romp with two startling double stops of C♯/A (7th/5th) and F♯/C♯ (3rd/7th) that create a cornucopia of harmony over the sustained D chord.

Performance Tip: If picking with bare fingers à la Duane, use the right-hand thumb and index fingers to simultaneously pluck the double stops in measure 20.

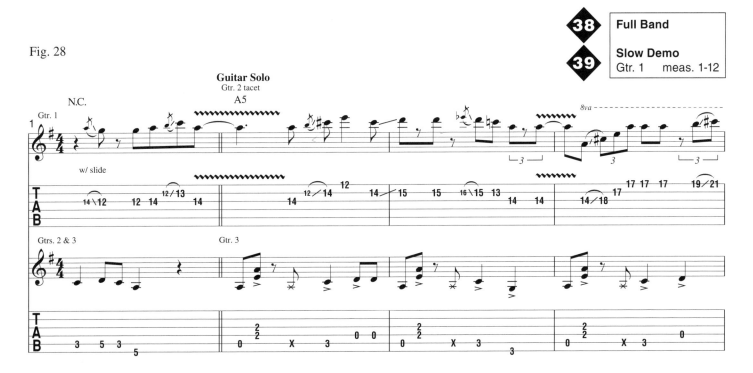

Fig. 28

38 Full Band

39 Slow Demo
Gtr. 1   meas. 1-12

Trouble No More (Someday Baby)

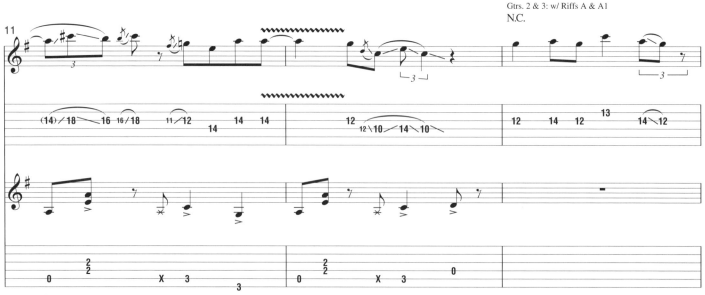

Trouble No More (Someday Baby)

WHIPPING POST

(*At the Fillmore*, 1971)
Words and Music by Gregg Allman

When Duane first heard the intro to "Whipping Post," he said to Gregg, "That's good, man. I didn't know you understood 11/4." Actually, it is in 11/8 time, but his point was made about Gregg's rhythmic creativity. It took the band the entire session on August 7, 1969, to track an acceptable recording. Like "Freebird," the extraordinary popularity of this song used to prompt fans to yell out requests for it at the concerts of other artists, including Frank Zappa, who saw the humor and finally learned it and performed it with his band in the eighties.

Figure 29—Intro

The one-measure "signature" intro riff of "Whipping Post," played by Duane (Gtr. 1), plays seven times following Berry Oakley playing it slightly different and unaccompanied two times. It consists of the root (A), ♭3rd (C), 4th (D), and ♭7th (G) notes derived from the A minor pentatonic scale with the addition of the ♭3rd bent one-half step to the major 3rd (C♯) as the final note. Though simple in concept, the sixteenth-note phrasing in 11/8 time creates a memorably springy line previously unheard of in rock music.

Performance Tip: Use the ring and index fingers for the A and G notes on string 6. Considerable pressure will need to be applied to the pull-offs, because the A note is only picked once for each six-note grouping. A good way to increase the volume of the pull-offs is by scraping the ring finger across the A note rather than lifting straight up and off.

Fig. 29

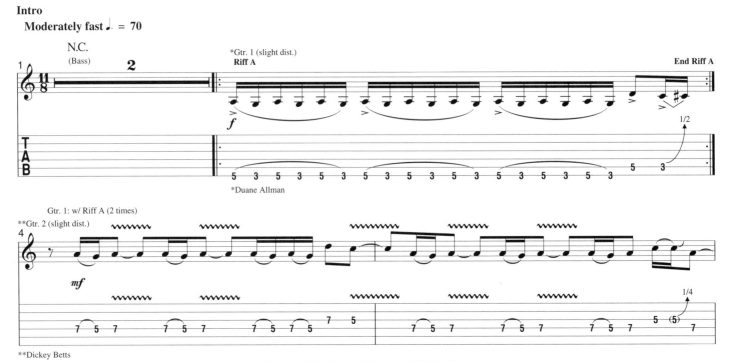

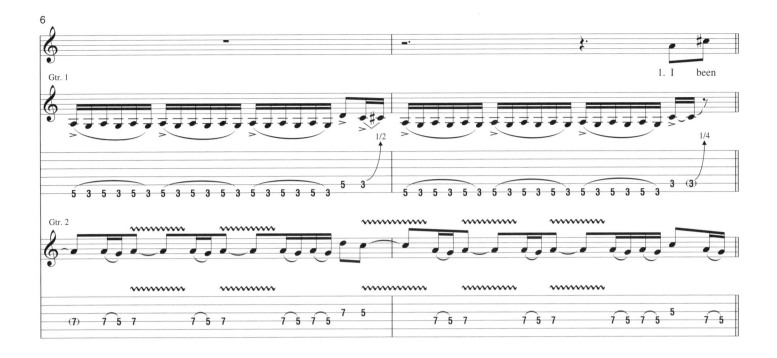

Figure 30—Chorus

The 11-measure chorus shifts from the verse's 6/8 time (not shown) to a bluesy 12/8 time through measure 7. A dramatic degree of uplift and release is provided in contrast to the verse changes that produce consistent musical tension.

Over measures 1 and 2 of the IV7 (D7) and V7 (E7) changes, Duane (Gtr. 1) plays soaring fills in root position of both the D and E composite blues scales, respectively. Dig how, after resolving to the root (D) in measure 1, he bends the 9th (E) to the ♭3rd (F) and then the major 3rd (F♯), to define the major tonality, before seamlessly advancing up to fret 12 for solid resolution to the root (E) on beat 4. In measures 3–5, Duane and Dickey (Gtr. 2) join forces for gorgeous, fluid, twin-guitar harmony lines in 3rds of one measure each, drawn from the A composite blues scale. After resting in measure 6 (implied ♭III = C), Duane and Dickey return with a twin-guitar line in octaves derived from the A minor pentatonic scale, designed to mimic Gregg's last vocal line of, "...good Lord, I feel like I'm dyin.'" The exquisite blues phrasing, bending, and note selection complement the content of the vocals and also facilitate the smooth transition into measures 8–11, where it shifts to churning 11/8 time and features Duane and Dickey playing harmony in 5ths. Check out how they wisely construct their twin lines from the A Dorian mode over the I (Am), ii (Bm), and ♭III (C) chords comped by Gregg on his big B3 organ. Also note how this section of the chorus blends beautifully into Duane's solo that follows.

Performance Tip: In measure 7, bend the 4th (D) on string 2 at fret 15 with the ring finger backed up by the middle and index fingers. Bend the root (A) on string 3 at fret 14 by pushing up with the middle finger.

Fig. 30

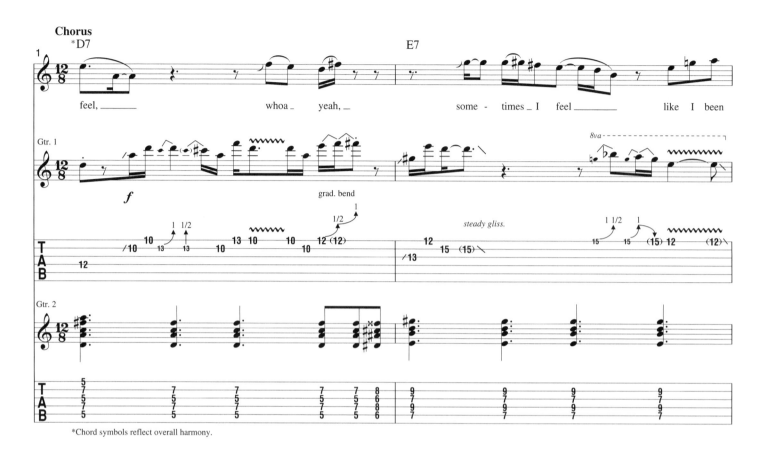

Chorus
*D7 ... E7

feel, _____ whoa_ yeah, _ some - times _ I feel _____ like I been

Gtr. 1

Gtr. 2

*Chord symbols reflect overall harmony.

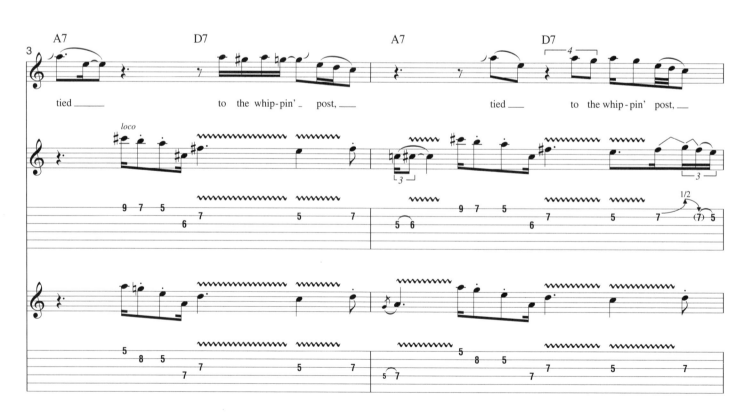

A7 ... D7 ... A7 ... D7

tied _____ to the whip-pin' post, _ tied _____ to the whip-pin' post, _

tied ___ to the whip-pin' ___ post, ___ good Lord, ___ I feel like I'm dy - in'.

Figure 31—Guitar Solo

Back in rolling 6/8 time, Duane (Gtr. 1) breaks into another electric guitar dimension for 129 measures of improvisational bliss. Similar in approach to the other modal extravaganzas like "In Memory of Elizabeth Reed" and "Mountain Jam," he uses his exceptional intuition and his trip hammer chops to forge a high-speed musical excursion of exhilarating peaks and deep valleys with a satisfying arrival at a surprising destination.

His first major stop in the A Dorian mode over the two-measure vamp of I (A)–ii (Bm)–♭III (C)–ii occurs right at the beginning of the solo. In measures 1–6, Duane helps establish the harmony by highlighting prime chordal and scale tones. For example, he punishes the tonic (A) in measure 1 and plays the 3rd (E) of C and ♭3rd (D) of Bm in measure 2. In measure 3, he gets on the root (B) of Bm, while in measure 4 he addresses the 5th (G) of C and the ♭7th (A) of Bm for musical tension. The 5th (E), ♭7th (G), and root (A) identify the A tonality while the 5th (F♯) of Bm creates forward motion in measure 5. The 3rd (E) reappears over the C in measure 6, while the ♭3rd (D), 9th (C), and ♭7th (A) extend the harmony of Bm, along with producing musical anticipation.

In measures 17–23, Duane begins incorporating various blues bends to hike up the energy, including the funky double-string harmony of D/A (4th/root) to E/B (5th/9th) on beat 1 of measure 23 that functions as the 4th/root of Bm on beat 4. Starting on measure 26 through measure 28, he handles one of his classic improvisational tools with a stutter-string descent down string 2; the purpose is to take him to a new place in the open position in measures 29–34, where twisting, multiple pull-offs of B–A–G and F♯–A–D provide dynamic contrast of register and phrasing. Without a noticeable break in action, Duane heads right back up the scale in measures 35–36 to take him to measures 37–51, where a barrage of whining, unison, and rich harmony bends build compressed tension while providing texture in contrast to all the quick, clean, single notes that precede them. With measure 52 functioning as a transition measure, Duane jolts the progression in measures 53–55 with quicksilver triplet pull-offs from C to A, then E. Speaking of transitions, do not miss the unison bends in measures 58–60 of G, A, A♯, B, D, and E (with the A♯ as a chromatic passing tone) that lead to languid glisses and sustained/vibratoed notes as the energy is dynamically throttled back in measures 61–76.

In measures 77–84, Duane drops dramatically and even more dynamically to the lower register on the bass strings in root position of the A minor pentatonic scale as a prelude to the dyads in 4ths, 6ths, and 5ths of measures 88–104 that send his solo into overdrive as the climax of this rocket ride. He starts out in measures 88–90 with C/G and C/A dyads alternating briskly to create yet another level of hefty harmony and tension before the big musical statement of the mandolin-strummed 5ths, ascending and descending the scale, that follow. In measures 113–128, he begins downshifting with far fewer notes per measure, progressively longer vibrato, and slithery glisses as the end of his fret-burning trip is in sight. Still creating like crazy in measures 129–132, Duane goes out strumming sparkly A octaves at a lower, cleaner volume that hook up logically and directly with the A, Bm, and C changes of verse 2 (not shown).

Performance Tip: Play the octaves in measures 129–132 with the index and pinky fingers, while the index mutes string 2 by lightly touching it with the flat, fleshy part of the pad.

Fig. 31

*Switch to bridge pickup.

*Played behind the beat.
**Switch to neck pickup.

2. My friends

Gtr. 1

Gtr. 2

YOU DON'T LOVE ME

(At the Fillmore, 1971)
Words and Music by Willie Cobbs

"You Don't Love Me" is the fourth classic blues cover on *Live at the Fillmore,* in addition to "Statesboro Blues," "Done Somebody Wrong," and "Stormy Monday," whose epic rendering of the atypical 27-measure progression at 19:16 is the second longest track after the 23:03 of "Whipping Post." On an album famous for featuring Duane in all his magnificence, it is perhaps the finest testament to his standing as one of the greatest post-war electric guitarists of all time.

Figure 32—Intro

Duane (Gtr. 1) makes clear his intent from the get-go that this is going to be his show and that he is going to shine and burn in the spotlight at every opportunity. For 41 measures, he improvises on the four-measure signature riff in the root position of the A blues scale. In measures 1–8, he grooves unaccompanied, save for the enthusiastic hand claps of the audience who joined in at his request of, "Put your hands together for this." Dickey (Gtr. 2) begins playing similar patterns in measures 9–17, at which point a drummer (Butch?) enters with just his kick drum, continuing through measure 25 when the rest of the band jumps in. The trick in this situation is to break free from the confines of the basic pattern without halting the momentum. Duane accomplishes this goal with consummate skill in measures 7 and 8 by employing time-warping bends in measures 17, 19, and 37, with D (IV) and C (♭III) triads that stimulate the senses both rhythmically and harmonically.

Performance Tip: In measures 4, 12, 24, 28, 32, 36, and 40, play the E (5th), E♭ (♭5th), and D (4th) notes with the ring, middle, and index fingers, respectively. In addition, also use the index for the C (♭3rd) at fret 3, pulling down for the quarter-step bend to the "true blue note."

Full Band

Fig. 32

*Duane Allman   **Chord symbols reflect basic harmony.

***Played behind the beat.   †Played ahead of the beat.

**Played ahead of the beat.

*Gtr. 2 (clean)

*Dickey Betts

You Don't Love Me

Figure 33—Guitar Solo

Duane blasts out of the gate and roars down the track through two 27-measure choruses of IV7 (D7, four meas.), I7 (A7, five meas.), IV7 (four meas.), I7 (five meas.), V7 (E7#9), IV7, I7 (six meas.) each. Of great significance is the fact that the progression begins on the IV chord and repeats that change in measures 10–13, thereby creating strong forward motion back to the I chord that follows. Of course, Duane is all over the situation by acknowledging the chord changes, including the V chord, through his shrewd note selection from the composite blues scale.

As Duane sears his way through the 54 measures, he uses various scale positions almost as motifs; this can be seen most prominently over the I7 (A7) chord in measures 14–16, 31–33, and 40–43, where he mostly hangs out in the Albert King box of the A minor pentatonic scale. The purpose of this choice seems to be the ease of accessing the root (A) on string 2 at fret 10, along with the ♭7th (G) leading tone two frets lower to add the blues tinge.

For the IV7 (D7) change, Duane finds that the unnamed "box" around the 12th position allows him to manufacture steaming, hot musical tension in measures 10–12 and 27–30. The main "hot lick" consists of the root (D) at fret 15 on string 2 bent one step to the 9th (E), while the 4th (G) at fret 15 on string 1 is fingered. The resulting G/E double stop "howls" like a banshee with extended dominant harmony that Duane resolves handily to the root.

Over the V7 (E7#9) and IV7 changes in measures 19–22, Duane uses "old reliable," the root position of the A minor pentatonic scale, mostly to create tension with bluesy scale tones and a judicious use of root notes. In measures 45–48, due to the increased "heat" generated by his powerfully-charged phrasing and attack, Duane decides to boost his location up an octave to fret 17 for a high "altitude" finish. Be aware that measures 21–22 and 47–48 of the IV chord are actually measures of rest with the harmony implied, and that Duane prudently gooses the forward motion with snappy pull-offs as to not slack off the forward motion. After dipping back into the signature I-chord riff in measures 59–60 of the I7 chord for resolution however, he floors it one more time by climbing up the scale with a series of unison bends of the 5th (E), root (A), ♭3rd (C), 4th (D), 5th (E), and octave at fret 17 in a cool move that he keeps in his arsenal for the right moment.

Performance Tip: Play the siren-like dyads at fret 15 over the IV chords by bending the D note with the ring finger backed up by the middle and index finger, while holding down the G note with the pinky.

Fig. 33

You Don't Love Me

Figure 34—Free Time

Twenty-two measures into his second guitar solo, Duane (Gtr. 1) silences the rest of the band in a manner similar to the concert stylings of tenor saxophone legend John Coltrane, and precedes to "blow" his "horn" completely unaccompanied for 41 astounding measures. As opposed to what many lesser "guitar heroes" would do in the sixties and seventies in copycat situations, he pointedly does not exploit the opportunity to strut his vaunted chops. Rather, Duane reaches deep inside and bares his soul with a wordless musical story full of bittersweet, lyrical, and melodic lines, as well as dramatic pauses, and dynamic shifts in register and phrasing.

Though no chords are played or indicated, Duane proceeds as if in the key of A major and, with few exceptions, he mines the A minor pentatonic scale in a variety of positions. When in the B.B. King box at fret 10, however, he does resort to including the 6th (F♯) and the 9th (B) on string 2 at fret 12 from the A major pentatonic scale, sometimes referred to as the F♯ minor pentatonic by blues guitarists; this can be seen right off in measures 3–6 of fluid, languorous phrasing where he routinely bends the 9th up to the major 3rd (C♯) for the purpose of subtly injecting an idea of major tonality among the preponderance of ♭3rd (C) and ♭7th (G) blues notes. Also, check out how he often follows the 3rd with the root (A), as on beat 2 of measure 4, to firmly anchor the implied A major harmony.

Starting in measure 10, Duane eases on down the road to root position of the A minor pentatonic scale where he begins to take his solo in another direction with more "edge" by bearing down harder on the strings. In measures 11–13, he hints at a call-and-response to come by creating tension with the 4th (D), being repeatedly bent one step to the 5th (E) on string 3, and resolved to the root on string 4 at fret 7. Getting "down and dirty" for a dynamic respite from the high-register riffing, he skips nimbly on the bass strings in measures 15–21 while engaging in "call" with notes like the ♭3rd (C) bent a quarter-step to the "true blue note" on beat 1 of measure 16. He follows with a "response" with the 5th (E) on beat 1 of measure 17 as both the C and E notes actually produce musical tension without resolution. The concept is to keep the focus moving forward, of course. Observe how he uses a snaky, little, bass-string riff that ends on the 4th (D) on beats 1 and 2 in measures 15 and 21 as a motif, along with a similar one that ends on the 5th in measures 16–17. These compositional "signposts" are important to have in any solo and are invaluable in this situation where structure is critical in order to avoid the pitfall of sounding like one is mindlessly "noodling."

As Duane dynamically "edges" back up the scale into a higher range, he plays a new motif four times in measures 25–27, that is loosely based around the ♭3rd (C), root (A), 5th (E), and ♭7th (G) notes. Building upon the anticipation created, he advances his musical goal, beginning in measure 28, with repetition and vibrato of the 4th (D) on string 1 at fret 10. Also known as the "suspended 4th," it is a powerful improvisational tool to build tension and is effectively worked through measure 34. In measures 35–38, he begins to up the ante, energy-wise, with more notes along with convoluted licks and bends. He maintains attention on the 4th in the root position of the A minor pentatonic scale with bends ranging from microtones (three-quarters of a step) to whole-step bends. Finally in measure 39, he runs back down to the bass strings, ending on the root (A), on string 6 at fret 5, that he cascades one step to the 2nd (B) in measure 40, 1-1/2 steps to the ♭3rd (C), and then a heroic two steps to the major 3rd (C♯). He releases and logically resolves the roaring bass-string frequency back to the root, on beat 1 of measure 41, where he vibratos it for the duration of the measure to the applause and relief of his mesmerized audience at the Fillmore.

Performance Tip: The only possible way to bend the root on string 6 to that degree is by pulling down with the ring finger with assistance from the middle and index fingers.

47 **Full Band**

Fig. 34

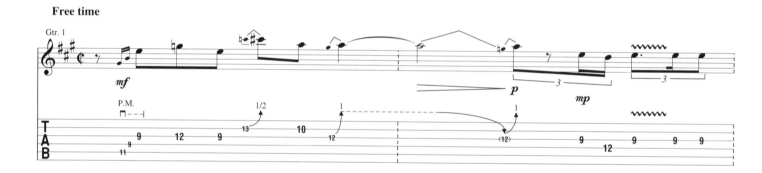

　　　　　　　　　　　　　　　　　　　　　　　　You Don't Love Me